THE JERUSALEM SYNDROME

MY LIFE AS A
RELUCTANT MESSIAH

MARC MARON

BROADWAY BOOKS NEW YORK

BROADWAY

Broadway Books titles may be purchased for business or promotional
use or for special sales. For information, please write to:
Special Markets Department, Random House, Inc.,
1540 Broadway, New York, NY 10036.

PRINTED IN THE UNITED STATES OF AMERICA.

BROADWAY BOOKS and its logo, a letter B bisected on the diagonal,
are trademarks of Broadway Books, a division of Random House, Inc.

Visit our website at www.broadwaybooks.com

LIBRARY OF CONGRESS CATALOGING-IN-PUBLICATION DATA
Maron, Marc.
The Jerusalem syndrome: my life as a reluctant messiah / Marc Maron.
p. cm.
1. Maron, Marc. 2. Jewish comedians—United States—Biography.
3. Maron, Marc—Religion. I. Title
PN2287.M515 A3 2001
792.7'028'092—dc21
[B]   2001025989

Designed by Gabriel Levine

ISBN 978-0-7679-0810-8

10 9 8 7 6 5

This book is for my mother, Toby, who claims she did the best she could, and for my father, Barry, whose selfishness propelled me into the darkness.

WELCOME TO THE BOOK. MARC MARON HAS been brought to you by the following: Eastern Europe, a faulty diaphragm, Dr. and Mrs. Barry Maron, Similac (in 1963 women just didn't breastfeed), Gerber baby food, Sid and Marty Croft, Mark Twain Elementary School, Congregation B'nai Israel, Kellogg's Frosted Flakes, *Mad* magazine, Post Cereals' Cocoa Pebbles, Procter & Gamble, Johnson & Johnson, Crest toothpaste, Aquafresh toothpaste, until the novelty wore off and then Crest again, Swanson frozen foods, Highland High School's Class of '81, KQEO-AM, the American Broadcasting Company, the National Broadcasting Company, and whatever CBS stands for, the Rolling Stones—a division of Rolling Stone Records, a division of Columbia Records, Boston University Classes of '85 and '86, City Lights Books, *National Lampoon*, The Grateful Dead, cotton, poultry, beef—it's what's for dinner, pork—I know it's wrong but come on, bacon?—Anheuser-Busch, Pfizer, Eli Lilly and Co., Glaxo-SmithKline, Parke-Davis, Humboldt County, Mr. Pibb,

Jack Daniel's, several Third World dictatorships' co-caine, General Electric, Wendy's, General Dynamics, the Military Industrial Complex, the Museum of Modern Art, Schwinn, Hanes, Wisconsin cheese, Heinz Ketchup, The Comedy Store, Vivid Video, Clarke's desert boots, Fender guitars, Harvey Altman CPA, the Walt Disney Company, Philip Morris, Coca-Cola, Seagram's, United Synagogue Youth, 3 Arts Entertainment, the three branches of the United States Government, Nabisco, Rolling Rock beer from Latrobe Brewing Company, Latrobe, Pennsylvania, Time-Warner Inc., Universal Studios—an MCA company, Chess Records, Fed Ex, Sprint, HBO, Datsun, Beatrice, AT&T, Bill Graham Presents, the American Psychiatric Association, and Fruit of the Loom.

THE JERUSALEM SYNDROME

1

DURING the summer of 1998 my wife and I took a trip to Israel. I know what you're thinking: *Israel?* Is this going to be heavy? I understand. That's what our friends thought when we told them about our trip. When you tell people you are going to Israel it makes them nervous. It somehow implicates their lack of religion and they want to know why you're going. They get worried. "Are you going to get Jewy?"

They don't know what you're going to be like when you get back. People change. Am I going to walk off the plane davening down the gateway wearing a tallit and a yarmulke with *payes* bouncing beside my ears? Then they're going to think, *Now it's weird. We can't go to their house anymore, certainly not on Saturdays. That pretorn toilet paper thing gives me the creeps.*

We didn't go to Israel to get Jewy. We went because a friend of mine invited us.

It was only after we got back from Israel that I read about Jerusalem Syndrome. This is a psychological condition that occurs in some visitors to the Middle East. They get to Israel and just snap. They think they are a biblical or religious figure like Moses, Jesus, or Muhammad. Some think that they are in a direct communication with God on a one-to-one level. Some think that *their* being in the Middle East is one of the keys that unlocks the final unfolding, which is what I like to call Armageddon.

In retrospect, I'm pretty sure I had a full-blown case of Jerusalem Syndrome. The catch is, I actually think I had it long before I left. It's hard for me to tell, because I always felt like I was special.

I was the first child of my parents and the first grandchild for both sets of grandparents. So, needless to say, I was special. For my entire life, until the day she died a few years ago, my Grandma Goldy would pull me aside from the rest of the brood, look me in the eyes, smiling, and say, "Marc-y, you're my number one." Then she would slip me a piece of dietetic coffee candy.

The other reason I believe I'm special is mystical. I was born on Kol Nidre, the eve of Yom Kippur. It is the holiest night in the Jewish religion. It was 8:10 P.M., September 27, 1963. A somber mood rippled through the Judaic collective unconscious. Jews around the world were repenting for their sins in shame, guilt, and fear. They were all asking God to write their names into the book of life for one more year as I slid out of my mother, covered in blood and crying in a Jersey City hospital. What does it mean? I don't know, but Jesus was born on Christmas—what are the odds? And if there is any core to my faith at all it is in that there are no coincidences. [There is no word in Hebrew for "coincidence."] Nothing happens in God's world by chance.

My father-in-law, Marty, wanted to be a rabbi but instead became a psychiatrist, thus cutting out the middleman, God. I asked him if he had heard of Jerusalem Syndrome and told him the symptoms. He said he had never come across it but it sounded to him like a decompensating borderline personality disorder, paranoid schizophrenia with delusions of grandeur or mania, which is what I like to call the fun side of bipolarity. He was, all and all, very clinical.

Maybe if he had become a rabbi it would've been a longer conversation, had over a stack of sacred texts revolving around how God manifests himself in this world and how all Jews that follow the rules want and expect to

experience revelation. The Hasidim believe that all be-
haviors of people and all events, good or bad, are mani-
festations of God on Earth. They are put before us so we
may engage our free will and make a choice between life
or death, good and evil, God or self. This illustrates one
of the primary differences between Jews and Christians.
In the Christian texts the wages of sin is death. In the
Jewish texts the wages of sin are negotiable. There are
those of us who don't follow the rules.

I'm not a religious person. I was born in New Jersey. I
was raised in Albuquerque, New Mexico. My parents
were of the first generation of Jews to move as far away
from their parents as possible for reasons other than flee-
ing a country. They just had to get away. When people
ask me what I am, I tell them, "I'm a Jew but I'm not a
Jew."

2

BEFORE we left New Jersey we lived in Pompton Lakes with my grandparents, Jack and Goldy. My father was never around because he was busy finishing medical school and my mother was never around because she was busy trying to finish becoming herself—a project she is still working on. She was twenty-two when she had me. For my formative years my soul and being were in the care of my Grandma Goldy.

She was a tall woman with a charming smile that could disarm anyone in seconds. She talked to everyone everywhere about everything in her life that made her proud, which was usually me. When Grandma looked down at me and smiled, it was one of the only times I really understood what it felt like to be loved. Godly Goldy was the keeper of an eternal stash of melon balls, boiled chicken, and soup. To me this was the holy trinity. One of the only objects of hers I took after her death was her melon baller. I use it in the summer as a device to go back in time.

My Grandpa Jack was an average-size man with a protruding round belly, thinning white hair and a strange bump on his forehead. He looked like a Jewish Buddha. He was always curious about how things worked and he could seemingly fix just about anything, if he could find a screwdriver and his glasses. Finding Jack's glasses was a frequent activity and one of the rituals that bonded my grandparents. Jack's disposition wavered among engaged, irritated, and amused. He had a nasal giggle that could stop time because time wanted to let Jack laugh. When Jack smiled, everything within a fifty-foot radius of him smiled. When Jack yelled, the same things ran for cover. He was a powerful man.

During the day Jack sold televisions, air conditioners, washers, dryers, and dishwashers at his appliance store in Haskell. Had for years. He helped bring the hill people of that region, the Jackson Whites, into the age of electronic convenience and entertainment. He was an early emissary of illusion. At night and on weekends he would alternate between reading everything—magazines, newspapers, books—and watching TV. He fed on information. He could watch any sport with an equal amount of interest, whether it was football or curling. He knew enough about everything to have an opinion sufficient to converse intelligently in the time afforded him by commercial breaks. He would lie on his side on the sectional with his head on one of the cushions turned perpendicular to the back of the couch. He always had his arm pointing straight up into the air with his clicker in his hand like a divining rod. It looked uncomfortable to me, but maybe there was method to it. Maybe God was guiding his channel selection.

The television was mounted in a wall in the den. The back of the set jutted out into a closet. Sometimes I would go into the closet and stand behind the set and my grandpa would say, "I can see you on TV." We played that game often. I transcended channels. It was a lie I wanted to believe.

Next door to my grandparents lived the Nurik family: Irv, Marjie, Jody, Tracy, Cary, and Jeff. At one time or another they all baby-sat my brother, Craig, and me and they had a pool, so we were over there often. Irv was a hyperintelligent man, obsessed with film. He had shelves crammed with books about movies. I couldn't stop looking at those books. There were stills from films I had never seen set beside formal portraits of the actors in them. To me, they were portraits of magicians capable of conjuring perfect realities. I became fascinated with the black and white faces of Hollywood's Golden Age. I could name them like some kids could name baseball players. I didn't know what Tom Seaver looked like, but I could identify Lionel Barrymore at a distance.

Deep within the Nurik house was a cave of enlightenment that permanently changed the way I looked at the world. The first time Cary baby-sat us, I remember walking through a hallway in their house, then up some stairs into a small dark room that seemed to resonate with a compelling weirdness. Cary was a bearded teenager and the keeper of a mystical domain. The walls and ceiling of his room were entirely covered with posters: an American Indian smiling with a sandwich ("You don't have to be Jewish to love Levy's real Jewish rye"), Zappa Crappa, The Fillmore, Procol Harum, Hendrix, the Marx Brothers smoking a hookah, W. C. Fields, Muddy Waters, and foldouts from *Crawdaddy* magazine. There were at least two thousand records lining every wall of the room. There were stacks of *Mad* magazines in the corner. Above his desk in a frame was the promotional lobby card of the cast of Tod Browning's *Freaks*. Irv's books and Cary's room singed themselves onto my cortex. They left a brand that marked a doorway to dark mysteries in my mind. Behind that door lay the isolated suffering of the human oddity, the enchanting, dark spell cast by celluloid royalty and the chaotic, drug-soaked spirituality of the sixties.

3

WE left New Jersey when I was seven and moved to Anchorage, Alaska, where my father did a two-year stint in the air force and my mother faded into a self-obsessing darkness.

Our next-door neighbor was a woman named Esther. She baby-sat us. My mother would walk us over to her house, and when the door opened the warm smell of cigarettes and stewing meat would engulf us. Her living room felt like the lair of a witch. It was always dark and eerily cluttered with Chinese, Japanese, and Eskimo artifacts and art. Everything was mysterious and delicate in Esther's house, including Esther. She looked like she was a hundred years old but had the energy and intensity of someone half that age. She would sit in a big chair in a cove by the door surrounded by shelves filled with little boxes, statuettes, books, and pieces of fool's gold. She had the air of royalty in exile. My brother and I would sit with her and she would smoke and tell us stories about bears and the beginning of time, which I believed she personally witnessed. She told us that God caused earthquakes and snowstorms to remind people who was in charge and that when people died God was bringing them home. It was the first I'd heard of this "God" idea.

Esther told us about her father, the pioneer, the westward expansion, and the construction of the railroad. Listening to Esther was like listening to a crumbling mountain or an emphysemic tree talk about what it had seen. Every so often her husband, a tall, quiet American Indian who always seemed to be wearing a jumpsuit, would come in and empty her ashtray. One day, after the stories, Esther pulled a box off the shelf, opened it, and took out two Liberty dollars from the 1800s. She gave one to my brother and one to me and then sent us home with some stew, a personal account of America's secret history, and the knowledge that God was in charge of death, destruction, and the weather.

My friend Chris, who had a cleft palate and no other friends, was my first partner in adventure. We set out after school on a Friday with our lunchpails and some paintings we had done in art class. We walked along the inlet over mounds of rubble that had been plowed there after the great earthquake of '64. We found tiles, shattered doorframes, and a fork, the residual artifacts of God's teachings. We lost track of the time and just kept walking until there was no more rubble, just a flat, barren dune that led up to a bridge that spanned the mouth of the inlet. There were a group of long-haired teenagers below the bridge cooking hot dogs on sticks over a campfire. How strange it must have been for them to see two seven-year-olds walk up out of nowhere with lunchboxes and artwork. They gave us each a stick and a wienie and told us to put the fire out when we were done. We watched them walk away and we ate the best hot dogs we had ever tasted. They were the hot dogs of freedom.

Chris and I were alone in the wilderness, and the sun was setting. We peed on the fire and walked up onto the bridge. It was a railroad bridge, and beyond it was nothing but water covered by a blanket of boulder-size chunks of ice for miles. We stood there looking for whales.

The sky was gray and the air was skin-stinging cold. I could feel the expanse of the land and water in my mind and the weight of being so close to the top of the world. The pressure of a magnetic pole and the axis of the planet pulled me open into that gray and it became a peaceful backdrop, an open-ended tone humming mystical and spiritual possibilities. I closed my eyes and took a deep breath, and then, through his nose, Chris said, "We are in so much trouble."

We *were* in trouble, but to this day that Gray comes over me. It is an inner retreat that opens when the fragments of memory of every second of my life contract together in those flashes of eternity triggered by a smell or a sound or another person or just a moment when the doors of the train open into the air. It usually happens on crisp fall days at the onset of winter. There is a dull burst in my chest, a fleeting wholeness that fills me, and I am transported to the top of the world, where I stand alone and become the only connection between sky and Earth in a private audience with the idea of God.

The morning we were jolted awake by the house shaking, my father ran into our room and pulled my brother and me out of our bunk beds and into the cold morning air. Craig and I were in our pajamas. My dad was in his underwear and my mom was in her nightie. We all stood beneath the front doorframe. My father insisted that it was the safest place to be while the plates of the Earth shifted below us. Everything in my line of vision shook to the deep rumble. It was only a tremor, and no one was hurt. It was scary and awe-inspiring to feel completely out of control while God showed off.

I wasn't convinced that doorframes were safe. You should be in or out.

We were far from New Jersey, and going back to visit was a harrowing event. My father booked us on an air force cargo flight that left in the middle of the night—I guess because it didn't cost him. That plane was the biggest plane I've ever been in. A few seats lined the sides of the fuselage, and there were only a few other passengers on the plane, mostly military people, along with stacks of crates and these strange-looking rectangular boxes.

The pilot invited my brother and me into the cockpit. He showed us the controls of the plane and explained the radar screens. He told us that the rectangular boxes in the back held the bodies of soldiers being sent home from Vietnam. When we sat back down and strapped ourselves into our seats against the wall, I felt the dense deep fear from sharing space in the air with death. I pictured soldiers and war. I thought about God bringing them home and men who could fly ships at night guided by blips of light carrying a cargo of stories that ended in boxes of shattered remains. It was all so overwhelming that I cried at the thought that I could die. A living soldier told me it would be alright and gave me a boxed meal of a sandwich, a banana, some cookies, and a V-8. It was the first time I ever drank a V-8. It was an adult drink and it was good. Now when I see a can on a grocery shelf, it's like a psychic trigger: V-8, almost eight years old, Vietnam, death, God's cargo, a box of food.

I have no recollections of my Jewishness in Alaska, other than knowing that I was a Jew and getting in trouble for drawing a picture of Hitler in Hebrew school. Not that I knew who he was or what he did. I had just seen pictures of him in a book and his mustache made him easy to draw. The swastika was an enchanting, brain-twisting symbol and also very easy to draw. I liked to draw. My drawings made grown-ups mad.

4

THE first time I had actual words with God, he started it. We moved to Albuquerque in 1972. My mom, my dad, my brother, myself, and an old English sheepdog named Mac crammed into a Caprice station wagon and drove down the Pacific Coast Highway. Buddy Holly's "That'll Be the Day" blared through the back speakers and my father was laughing and singing. *Buddy Holly: A Rock 'n' Roll Collection* was his favorite eight-track. We heard it over and over again. He told us Holly had been killed in a plane crash at the peak of his powers. I would stare at the picture on the tape, trying to connect the man with the voice and the horrible end he met. For years the human manifestation of death in my mind wore black horn-rimmed glasses. It was also then I realized that sometimes God took some people home for being too damn good.

My brother and I would lie out in the back bed of the station wagon and look out the rear window, up at the clouds. It happened as we drove through the Arizona desert. I don't know if I was in waking consciousness or if it was a dream, but I saw this huge guy standing over the clouds with his arms crossed like someone overseeing fieldwork. He was about the size of the Jolly Green Giant. He had no shirt on and he was wearing satiny Turkish-looking pants that ruffled in the wind like a hot-air balloon being inflated. I couldn't see his face because there was pure light emanating from it and a cloud in the way, but he looked like a giant genie. It was clear to me at that moment that he was God, the grand instigator of earthquakes, snow, and death. As I remember, I was squinting, trying to see his face, and I heard a booming voice say, "What are you looking at? What are you going to do about it?" He was challenging me. That was the moment I was infected with Jerusalem Syndrome.

"I don't know," I said. "I'm eight."

Then the montage of roadside signs flew by on the sides of the car and my consciousness: McDonald's, Arby's, 7-Eleven. Civilization, context, consistency, food.

Then my brother yelled, "McDonald's, McDonald's, let's go to McDonald's."

Eight years old, eight-tracks, rock 'n' roll, death, and God in the desert.

Once we got planted in the Land of Enchantment, being a Jew became a part of my life. My father opened his medical practice and worked. My mother went back to school and painted pictures. There were other Jewish families in Albuquerque, and in time we got to know most of them. Most of us went to the same synagogue and all the kids went to the same Hebrew school, which is where I began to understand my unique talent for driving people to the edge. In my mind, the entire Hebrew school concept had nothing to do with learning about Judaism. It was there to let me blow off the steam and rage that accumulated in my being during regular school. Why not? It just seemed that there was less on the line. So what if they kicked me out of Hebrew school? What could happen? I wouldn't be allowed to be a Jew? So, twice a week, at four in the afternoon, I would go to Congregation B'nai Israel and redefine the phrase "the Jewish problem."

I verbally abused the teachers, constantly cracked jokes, and cussed. I generated as much anarchy as possible via spitballs, farts, fights, and preadolescent sexual outbursts. I was very proud to have pushed two of my Hebrew school teachers to tears. One of them actually quit because of my behavior. I relentlessly made fun of this kid who sat in the back of the room picking his nose with a crochet needle. I swear, he did it every Monday and Wednesday for three years, until one day he bled and had to be sent to the hospital. I mocked all rituals and traditions at every opportunity and I laughed during services.

The first time I got loaded was at a friend's bar mitzvah party in the social hall, after which I projectile-vomited all over the stall of the boys' room. The first time I smoked a whole cigarette was in the back parking lot of the temple with Herb, the gentile shul janitor from Brooklyn, who wore cowboy boots and told tales of pain about his ex-wife to dizzy twelve-year-olds. His entire face seemed to wrap around each draw on his filterless Camel. He resonated a reality of a life lived and left. Herb was the first heart-hardened man I ever knew and I listened to him because he let me smoke.

The only things I remember actually learning about Judaism and Hebrew prior to my bar mitzvah were that *kelev* meant dog, *adonai* meant God, your head had to be covered in the sanctuary, mezuzahs have a rolled-up piece of paper in them, Hitler and the Germans once bull-

dozed piles of dead Jews into holes and the ones they
didn't they made into soap and lampshades, Golda Meir
and the guy with the eyepatch were important in Israel,
and Jews were different from everyone else and that's why
nobody likes us. Holidays meant presents on Hanukkah;
honey-dipped apples on Rosh Hashanah; a long, draining meal on Passover, with symbolic crackers and questions during which we left the door open for a ghost to
come in and get drunk; no food and no school on Yom
Kippur (introducing the idea that all good things are
grounded in some kind of suffering); strange desert fruits
hung from the ceiling on Sukkoth; triangular prune
cookies shaped like a bad guy's hat for Purim. They were
delicious.

I studied for weeks preparing for my bar mitzvah. The
Torah reading was Deuteronomy 11:26–16:17 which
began with these words:

> *See, this day I set before you blessing and curse: blessing, if*
> *you obey the commandments of the Lord your God that I*
> *enjoin upon you this day; and curse, if you do not obey the*
> *commandments of the Lord your God, but turn away from*
> *the path that I enjoin upon you this day and follow other*
> *gods, whom you have not experienced.*

My haftorah was Isaiah 54:11–55:5, which began with these words:

Unhappy, storm-tossed one, uncomforted!
I will lay carbuncles as your building stones
And make your foundations of Sapphires.

I understood none of it then because it was in Hebrew and I don't remember ever reading it in English. Now it seems to prophesy my entire spiritual life.

I wore a light-blue leisure suit on Friday night and a navy three-piece suit on Saturday morning. My speech, as I remember it, was essentially an overview of my haftorah and what it meant to me, via the cantor who made me write it. It also included a long apology to the congregation for my past behavior. I was never confirmed and I wasn't convinced.

My Grandma Goldy gave me a gold-plated Elgin pocket watch to mark the occasion. The date 8-20-76 was engraved on the inside of the cover. My best friend, Dan, gave me an antique collapsible top hat and a cane. Show Time—high school—the need to belong and the quest to be different.

5

FRESHMAN year of high school I attended Sandia Preparatory. It wasn't *the* private school of the region, but it was the private school that the students who couldn't get into *the* private school went to. I had been at Sandia since seventh grade, and it took the faculty three years before they asked me to leave. My offenses ranged from the standard disruption of classes (pushing one elderly teacher to the point of slapping me in the face), cheating, smoking (which I was doing regularly—Marlboros, because Keith Richards smoked Marlboros), being sent home from a class trip after being caught with Patty Ryan's breasts in my hands, and general instigation of chaos. I believe that most of the teachers actually liked me because I was entertaining, but they had to do what was right for the school. A teacher whose last name was

Liberty rallied the faculty against me, and they asked me to leave after my freshman year. The letter said, "We suggest a military school or a boarding school for Marc. He possesses the wrong kind of leadership qualities." It was the best thing that could have happened to me. Liberty.

Public high school was really the most humbling punishment for a leader in exile. I went from a school with an easily led student body of 900 to a school of 3,400 students, and my power dissipated. The possibilities for a coup d'etat and the implementation of a clown junta were diminished. There is a freedom to anonymity. I became follower, a pupil, an adept of adolescent rebellion, and I joined forces with this guy named Dave because he had a car.

It was a 1971 gold Pontiac Firebird with a twin cam, a Holly double-pumping carb, and mag wheels. It could go 150 miles an hour. Dave had a reckless lack of fear that I admired and aspired to. He also had a compulsive, contagious laugh that made me want to be around him as much as possible. Dave's laugh made everything okay. We would go out on weekends and sit in front of liquor stores until we found someone to buy something for us. Dave drank beer and I drank Jack Daniel's because I didn't like beer. We would get ripped and drive around Albuquerque looking for girls and trouble. We rarely found girls. When Dave couldn't get into a fight, we would go to the parking lot of the Winrock shopping center (named for Winthrop Rockefeller, who was the developer) late at night and put shopping carts in front of the Firebird. We'd get them going about 60 miles an hour and let them slam into an embankment or a curb and watch them tumble into a mangled mess of chrome and wheels. I'd like to think of this as an early anticonsumerism action, an attack on the corporate elite, but it was really just pent-up sexual energy and rage.

Dave and I, along with my friends Bob and Brian, eventually got fake IDs. We were at a party, and there was a guy there making them. He had a large board that was an exact replica of a New Mexico driver's license. The corner was cut where the picture was supposed to be. Each of us held the board in front of our bodies and put our head in the corner. The guy stepped back a specific distance from the board. He judged the distance by a string he attached to the subject's foot. Then he shot a Polaroid. He would then give you the image and you took it home, trimmed it, and had it laminated. The only drawback was that he couldn't change the information on the board. We all had the same fake ID: same name, same height, same birthdate, same color eyes, and same Social Security number. We were a pack of Tom Bines. If we went to a bar, we would space ourselves between people going in and hope that the bouncer only looked at the birthdate. It usually worked.

Sometimes we would go to the Pyramid Theater on Central Avenue, which was the old Route 66. The front of the building, which faced Central, had a mural on it. It was a painting of a pyramid that had an eye in the top of it. It was set on a psychedelic background. There was a marquee above the eye that always said ADULT FILMS ALL NIGHT. The entrance of the theater was around the back. There was a small box office next to a room that had a beaded curtain and a sign on top of the door that said NUDE BODY PAINTING. We never asked any questions. We'd pay ten bucks and they wouldn't even card us. It was a small, dirty, musky-smelling place. There were probably forty seats, and no more than ten of them were ever occupied. You could smoke in there. It was where I saw sex for the first time.

I can't remember the name of the film, but it was a sixteen-millimeter feature. It opens with a guy on a bus pulling into a strange town. He meets a woman, and they end up at her place on her bed. She takes off his clothes. She takes off her clothes and on her belly is a tattoo of the Devil's face and the mouth and beard of the Devil is her vaginal region. During sex she kept screaming, "Fuck me.

Fuck the Devil. Fuck me. Fuck the Devil." The only other thing I remember is that the movie ends with a woman on all fours on an altar. She was naked except for a hood that covered her head, and there was a lit candle stuck in her ass. People holding candles wearing hooded robes surrounded her. They were chanting, "All hail Uranus. All hail Uranus." I don't really think the movie helped me in any way understand what needed to be done, but I've never forgotten it.

Sometimes on cold, clear winter days Dave and I would take the Firebird up old 14 behind the Sandia Mountains, cruising into the sun at 140 miles an hour, barely shaking. When the road bent west toward Santa Fe, the valleys and mesas spread out vast before us and the huge gold and orange sky was a wash of light that hit my face and shot right through to my soul. It made time stop and it made me feel like there was nothing better than being alive and in the world. I stashed that light beside the Gray in my heart as a companion.

Sophomore year I got my own car, and Dave and I became distant. I got a job at a restaurant called The Posh Bagel. It was owned by a balding, morally bankrupt, twenty-five-year-old obsessive-compulsive, nail-biting, Jewish New Yorker who looked forty. His name was Eddie Waxman. I learned much under his tutelage within the secular confines of his New York Jewish theme restaurant. It was directly across from the University of New Mexico. I was fifteen when I became a shift manager. I learned how to count out a drawer and cook on a grill. I learned how to smoke pot and do cocaine. I learned how to hate my boss and focus my subversion. It was like an advance placement in noncurricular activities, which is where I excelled.

There was a constant influx of lunatics into The Posh Bagel on a day-to-day basis. There was Pete, who always wore shorts and lace-up boots to his knees. He would sit and smoke Winchester cigarillos like they were cigarettes and draw pictures of guns with schizophrenic poem headings that I believed at the time implied a deep wisdom. There was Sunshine, who seemed to have gotten lost on his way home from Woodstock. It was then 1979, so he looked real lost. He had long, tangled blond hair and a beard and mustache. He wore ripped-up jeans and accessorized himself with no less than twenty scarves that hung from him in different places like he was a display rack for used scarves. Sunshine didn't speak. There was a guy we called Tree Man, because he was tall and the hair of his beard was matted together with the hair on his head by a green grime that covered his entire body and had a foliage-like quality to it. I was fascinated with the insane. Their uniqueness and their fragmented attempts to make sense of the world intrigued me. I thought they possessed the keys to understanding.

There were the students, my coworkers, and my teachers. There was Mike, one of the managers, who once took three Quaaludes before he counted the money and found that he couldn't count the money and all he wanted to do was mop the floors, which he did with a goofy, waltzing carelessness for two hours. I counted the money. There was John G, who insisted on putting sliced-up hot dogs in the vegetarian minestrone soup. There was Tracy and her boyfriend, Hugs, and their VW bus. There was the arrogant chef with sideburns, who came to work tripping on mushrooms and invented the best salsa I ever tasted. There was Judson, with his strange teeth and punk band. There was Suzanne and her birthmark, and Frances the bitch. There was Anna and her sad eyes, and Laurie the Latina.

I didn't know it at the time, but Eddie offered the waitress staff a bonus to the first one who took my virginity. So, the first time I got laid was by a waitress named Diamond. It was awkward, but a relief to get it out of the way. I guess that's a jewel.

Budget Records was next door to The Posh Bagel. A guy named Steve LaRue managed it. He was a frustrated musician who played in a two-man experimental rock band called Jungle Red with a guy named Craig. They only played out twice a year, intentionally. I would spend hours in the record store with Steve. He shook me out of my commercial rock brainwash and threw me into the lexicon of experimental art music: Fripp, Eno, Fred Frith, Jon Hassel, The Residents, and a whole world of avant-garde noise noodling.

The night I went to see one of Jungle Red's semiannual performances I had been out drinking with some high school friends and I told them we were going to an art party over by the college. We got to the house near the campus and rang the bell. When the door opened, there was a man wearing a loincloth with the word HEATHEN written across his chest in lipstick, standing in the doorway. He threw his hands in the air as if presenting something on the ceiling and said, "Welcome."

I think we said, "Uh, where's the keg?"

The house was packed with the cutting edge of the Albuquerque art scene. Mostly gay guys, women in black, and a few people that looked like they might've been part of the *A Flock of Seagulls* entourage. The stage was set. There were a couple of guitars next to a keyboard. One of the guitars had a doll's arm gaff-taped to the neck. Steve and Craig came out in surgical scrubs and proceeded to create a wall of chaotic sound. Steve was screaming and playing guitar, and Craig rocked back and forth, with his hands pounding the keyboard. Every few beats Steve would kick the guitar with the doll's arm taped to it, causing a feedback that was deafening. In the middle of the performance Steve pulled out a box of vintage Fiestaware that he had been collecting for years, and in between lyrics he would violently break a piece with a hammer. Beneath the din of electric noise was the sound of delicate colorful plates, pitchers, and cups being shattered by Steve's swift hand. As each piece fell into shards on the floor, one could hear a barely audible chorus of gay men groaning. It became an integral layer of the sound. It was an amazing show. Pure anger-infused rock 'n' roll art that engaged and disturbed people. There was Truth there. I wanted in.

The times, they were a changin'. The great war between disco and rock raged on the high school campus. Punk had surfaced as a legitimate disposition, and the freaks made some space available beside their perch for the new adolescent archetype. Soon after, new wave infused itself into the student population, so thin ties and poofy hair bobbed down the halls beside flannel-shirted long hairs, mohawks, and Britannia jean–clad dance-club kids. My sense of humor allowed me to walk freely through all the sectors. I had shifted my interests to the art department, where I immersed myself in the craft of photography. I played guitar. I began writing poetry. I no longer thought of myself as a high school student. I was an Emerging Artist.

My most important body of work was a series of photographs that won the Best of Show honor in the Highland High School Art Exhibition. I had set up a ladder in the middle of a three-acre field of freshly tilled sod. I set three female torso mannequins in the sod leading up to the ladder. I set the camera on a tripod. With the help of my mother (who was always supportive of my creative ventures) I put together a series of photographs of me approaching the ladder carrying a television set that was plugged into a work light I had hanging from my belt. The TV was on. The last few photographs are of me leaving the TV beside the ladder, climbing the ladder, jumping off the ladder, and me frozen in midair as if I were flying away. The very last image is the television set on top of the ladder, alone and on, replacing me, a private audience with the idea of God.

I made my headquarters the Frontier Restaurant on Central Avenue, down the street from The Posh Bagel. It was a huge Western theme restaurant that was famous for its homemade sweet rolls. It was the equivalent of an all-night diner, the meeting place of the dispossessed of all kinds. Some of my friends believed it was the center of the universe and would argue that point scientifically.

Around the corner from the Frontier was The Living Batch Bookstore and its proprietor, Gus Blaisdell. Gus was an intense, bearded man, a renegade intellectual with a dark past that included Stanford, two ex-wives, and alcohol. Sometimes he wrote books, sometimes he taught film at the university. He knew all the artists in the area and he knew everything about everything. He could reference art, literature, philosophy, mathematics, and theology with wit and bile. The Batch was his center of operations, but the Frontier was where he held court with professors, photographers, painters, writers, and washups. When I began talking to him I was a junior in high school and very intimidated, but he accepted me, most of the time. We have a correspondence to this day. He was the smartest, funniest man I had ever met and I aspired to his level of brilliance. He inspired me to understand. I wanted to be jaded. He also made me want to go to college, which I wasn't planning on doing.

I scrambled to get into a school. I wanted to get out of town. I wanted to go to Boston. It was two thousand miles away from my parents, and there were hundreds of colleges in the region. I thought one of them would accept me. My grades were shit other than in art-related classes and English. My senior year I actually did homework to get my GPA up, but it was too late. The only colleges that accepted me were Bunker Hill Community College and Curry College. I chose Curry, a small liberal arts school outside of Boston that was known for programs designed for dyslexic students and its lenience in accepting entitled high school fuck-ups. The slight difference in symptoms is sometimes difficult to discern, but I was definitely in the latter group.

6

I'VE never *really* practiced Judaism, I've never *really* believed in or had faith in the Jewish God or any God. I never *really* believed in *anything* other than self-expression and the deep desire to understand. I didn't think I needed to believe in anything else. Within a month of being at Curry, a black sheep from a rich European family named Rene introduced me to the work of the Beats. I began to read them and I saw a way I could engage all of my desires: rebellion, expression, intoxication, the search for answers, and individuality. The gates of Heaven opened and I looked inside. It was surprisingly dark, and all the angels were snapping their fingers to a walking bass line. Finally, something to believe in. I didn't want to be a Jew. I wanted to be a Bohemian. A

Beatnik. Theirs was a religion I could have faith in. And it was a religion.

There are the sacred texts. *On the Road* by Jack Kerouac covers the ritual elements of the religion. *Naked Lunch* by William Burroughs covers the moral and the metaphysical elements of the religion, and *Howl* by Allen Ginsberg covers the gay poetry elements of the religion. All religions have a gay poetry element. I urge you to read the Song of Solomon in the Old Testament with a lilt in your voice. You will find that there is definitely a gay man behind that poem. It just wasn't as popular to be an out gay poet in the time of King David.

There are tenets to the Beat religion. It is a spiritual system built on searching, pushing the limits, embracing life, being awake and wasted to be aware, being Beat, freeing your mind, questioning everything. The path of excess leads to the palace of wisdom. Nothing is true and everything is permitted. To be Beat is to be holy, man, and to be holy is to be closer to God. When asked by John Wingate on TV what exactly he was looking for, Jack Kerouac said, "I'm waiting for God to show me his face." Then he threw up on himself during a commercial.

There are rituals in the Beatnik religion. In order to partake in the rituals you must form a Bohemian crew.

This is essentially five to seven disenfranchised upper-middle-class white kids whose parents can afford to lay out forty thousand dollars for them to spend four years at college thinking they are Beatniks.

As for the rituals themselves, there must be coffee, cigarettes, and beer, you must read good poetry and write bad poetry and then read that aloud. You must smoke reefer and listen to jazz and stay up all night. There is also room within the Beat religion to call and ask your parents for money.

There must be deep philosophical discussions that go on for hours and hours about *nothing*. Every gathering must end at three or four in the morning with some drunken friend in your face yelling, "But you still haven't proven that you exist, man."

"Well, I'm tired, drunk, and high. I'm going to sleep now. Let's see if I exist tomorrow. Don't climb into bed with me again. It makes me uncomfortable."

That's another ritual. There must be two or more awkward sexual situations with two or more people that don't really culminate in anything but one person crying, "Am I gay? I think I'm gay." Then it's not really a sexual situation as much as it's a baby-sitting crisis.

There must also be a few occasions when you look down into your palm at a very small square piece of paper with maybe a Disney character, Mr. Natural, or a star printed on it and say, "Are you sure you know the guy you got this from? It's cool, right? I am not afraid. I'm going to do it. You're going to hang out, right? 'Cause the last time I did this I forgot my name."

There are also pilgrimages within the Beatnik religion. Of course, any car ride with another person, music, reefer, and no real destination can be a Beatnik pilgrimage. Some turn out to be more important than others.

In order to go on the pilgrimages, you must choose your Beatnik brother from your crew. You must find your Jack or your Neal. My Jack was a guy named Jim. I met him during my freshman year of college. Jim was an Irish kid. He had long blond hair and wore a faded Levi's jacket that had a red and white yin and yang symbol on the back that he had hand painted there one night.

Jim was angry but sweet. He'd been in the Boston area all his life. His father lived in Cambridge and his mother lived in Brookline. He spent a good part of his childhood on Cape Cod. Jim liked to drink. At dorm room parties he would usually consume a six pack of Genesee Cream Ale as he railed about politics, rants that fell on the deaf ears of drunken dyslexics and party kids. Toward the end of the evening Jim would stand up, hammered, and break into a flawless Jim Morrison impression and sing the first verse of "Break On Through," then pass out on the floor. This was a ritual. The second part of the ritual was that all the people in the room would gather around Jim's body and draw on his face with a pen.

Jim would brood around the quad, chain-smoking Marlboros and ranting about the Vietnam War as if he had been there.

"Da Nang was a mistake, man. We shouldn't have *been* there, man. It wasn't our war, Marc."

"Jim," I would say, "you weren't there. You're twenty. It's 1982. Take it easy. It's over. I can still see the peace sign on your cheek."

Jim was the kind of kid who would go away for the weekend and come back three weeks later and say, "Uhm, we went down to the Cape and I lost my watch. What did I miss? Can I check out your notes, man?"

Jim was my running buddy. We made the pilgrimages. The most important was the pilgrimage to Jack Kerouac's grave. It was a beautiful fall day in Boston. The air had an electric chill. I called Jim and said, "We're going to visit Jack."

He said, "Alright, man, swing by."

I remember the Gray came over me. I was present, alive, in the moment, connected to all things.

(Author's instructions: Dim the lights in the room

you're in, put on Coltrane, and read this aloud, standing.)

> *We climbed behind the helm of a 1979 Honda five-speed,*
>   *foreign car,*
> *A heresy, not really Beat, but it was my dad's and it was*
>   *free.*
> *The mellow hum of Japanese machinery propelled us*
>   *toward our destiny.*
> *Boston to Lowell, all forty-five miles, we didn't fall asleep*
>   *once.*
> *We talked about art, politics, philosophy, and what to*
>   *have for lunch.*
> *We jammed to jazz and beat our hands on the dash. I*
>   *think we had made it through half of Coltrane's "A*
>   *Love Supreme" when we pulled onto the path*
> *to the angelic, holy, hipster cemetery and the tomb of St.*
>   *Jack.*

We were led to the gravesite by an ancient guide wearing a hat with earflaps. We assumed he was the caretaker.
He told us that it was the most popular grave in the
cemetery. When he spoke, the top plate of his dentures
would slip in his mouth. It looked like he had an extra set
of teeth where his tongue should've been. He said,

"Bobby Die-lin and Joan Bry-ez once came up to visit." When we got to the grave, we thanked him and he wandered away, kicking leaves off the path, talking to himself.

I think we had the same moment most pilgrims have at the grave of Kerouac. We gazed down at the headstone, awed to be in the presence of Jack. We were there to pay our respects. We were there because we drove there. We were there because part of our journey was to bear witness to the place where his journey ended. We were there to earn some Beat creds. My brain was trying to calculate significance, manufacture some meaning. My soul was a dry sponge craving to absorb some residual greatness out of the sod. I lit a joint, sucked in a deep hit, held it, and from my constricted throat I said, "You know what, man? We've gotta get on the road."

"Yeah," Jim said, "I know what you mean."

There was a moment of deep silence between us as I exhaled slowly and watched the smoke dissipate into the gray, cold air of Lowell.

"No, I mean *now*, I've gotta be back for class in an hour. It's Romantic lit and if I miss it again, I won't be able to major in English."

Sometimes pilgrimages have their limitations.

We left an offering at the grave because that's what you

do at the tombs of your heroes. We set a small bottle of gin in front of the headstone. Codependency doesn't need to stop just because someone's dead.

Freshman year I lived in a house owned by the college. It was called the Green House and it was the "art dorm." The concept was to put seven socially retarded creative people in one living environment in the hopes that by giving them the freedom to do their art, they wouldn't drop out and the money would keep flowing through the halls of higher education.

I was a poet; a very important poet.

I lived on the first floor and in the attic lived a huge angry Jewish girl with wild, frizzy hair. Her name was Nancy and I believe she was the modern manifestation of Lilith. I felt she was holding the house down, both spiritually and physically. She would hole up in her room and frantically write poetry. She would sit at her typewriter scowling and smoking, and somehow it would all come out flowers.

A watershed in my spiritual development took place one night in the Green House. I wasn't expecting it, but I had done the work. I was living the Beat ideal as best I could, and I was rewarded. I remember I barged into Nancy's room. I was a freshman, so I must have been pestering her.

"What are you writing, Nancy? What are you writing? I want to read it. Come on, let me read it. I want to write but I can't. I'm so high. I'm blocked. Let me see it Nancy, come on. I don't know what I should do."

Nancy looked up from her typewriter and flipped her mane of hair back with her hand with a momentum that started in her lower back and whipped her entire upper body around to reveal her face.

"I don't care what you do. Just get out of my room. You should go write, go sleep, go meditate. I don't care. Just go." Her hair fell and she refocused on her type-writer.

Something about meditating clicked in little Beat Marc's head. "I'll meditate. Yeah. I've never tried that."

So, I went down to my room. I turned off the lights. I put on this music that Steve LaRue had turned me on to. It used water as a percussion instrument. *Very deep*.

I got into what I thought was a lotus position and I guess I improvised a mantra. It was probably something like, "Fuck yes! Fuck yeah! Here we go! Inner peace! Bring it on! Whoo!"

I was breathing deeply. At that point in my life it was most likely anxiety-related hyperventilation, but I was breathing deeply nonetheless. I remember I was slowly rocking back and forth. *Then something started to happen.* I heard a high-pitched tone in my ears. It sounded like that noise that came out of the television when programming used to stop for the night. The color bars of the test pattern appeared, floating over my head in a blue mist. I felt myself rising up out of myself. I felt my inner self slowly disengage from my body and rise to the ceiling. There I was, hovering over my body, looking down at myself listening to very pretentious music. I felt that I was being drawn toward something eternal. I thought, *Hey, this is amazing. I could go anywhere. I'm gonna go look God in the face.*

That thought was followed immediately by *I might be in trouble here. What if I can't get back into my body? That would be awkward and I would miss class.* So, I jumped back into my body, *hard.* I got in. Thank God. Then I ran upstairs to Nancy's room and pounded on the door.

In one fluid motion Nancy whipped the door open, went into a hair flip, and screamed, "What, Marc?"

I was gasping and out of breath. "I just meditated like you suggested. I was sitting on the floor and I left my body and rose up to the ceiling and looked down on myself sitting on the floor."

Nancy took a drag off her cigarette and said, concerned and scolding, "Really? That's called astral projection. Don't fuck with that." Then she slammed the door in my face.

I knew that was the end of the first phase of my mystical training. It was a gift of enlightenment. I had pushed myself to the limit and I felt closer to some eternal truth. I knew there was something out there trying to reach me. At least on an astral level. I had a belief system in place and it was working for me. My Jerusalem Syndrome had become symptomatic. Sophomore year I transferred to Boston University.

During my four years at Boston University I was a true Beat adept. I took a course in existentialism during which, with the help of my professor, I erased myself completely and had to rebuild from scratch. I drank. I fell in love with a girl who was coming out of a relationship with a girl and learned the true deep fury of jealousy because I was in a position to be jealous of both sexes. I drank. I had threesomes and took drugs. I drank. I had a sexual identity crisis. I drank. I wrote poems and short stories and was an editor of the literary journal. I drank. I had a nervous breakdown. I drank. I wrote, directed, and acted in plays. I drank. I had sex with enough women to be hated in several social circles. I drank. I was a film critic for the newspaper. I drank. I wrecked a car. I drank. I started doing comedy because I thought it was the purest expression of truth. I drank.

Some way or another I managed to graduate *cum laude*. The two people that most changed the way I saw the world during my time at B.U. were Carl Chiarenza and Lauren Osmolski. Chiarenza taught a yearlong survey in the history of photography that focused on defining a reproduced image, the artistic integrity of the reproduced image, and how the corruption of reproducing technology could be used to create an illusionary reality that could overshadow reality itself. Lauren taught me how to fuck.

7

AFTER I graduated from college I decided I was gunning for the Buddha. I would be a Beatnik warrior in search of the truth, the real truth, the *deep* truth. So, I moved to Hollywood, where the truth remains well hidden. I should mention that I also wanted to be a star. Sometimes I forget to mention that because I think it undermines my credibility as a seer.

I got on the road and drove to California. I stopped off in Albuquerque to check in with my parents and friends and had a brief affair with a woman who'd recently divorced a CIA agent. I stopped by The Living Batch to tell Gus what I was doing. When I walked into the store I saw a poster on the bulletin board for a Beat conference at the Naropa Institute in Colorado. All the Beats that were still alive were going to be there: Ginsberg, Burroughs, Corso, Snyder.

"I gotta get up there for that," I said.

"Why would you want to go up there and see those geriatrics?" Gus asked. "I know those guys. It would be a bore." This was new information for me.

"You know them? Did you know Kerouac?"

"I met him once at a party in Berkeley."

I was excited.

"Really?" I said. "What was he like?"

"He was standing in a corner, drunk," Gus said, "with his arm around Neal Cassady, slurring 'Live like a tree, Neal.' "

It didn't matter if it was true or a joke. I understood.

Then Gus said, "Go do what *you're* going to do."

It was time for me to have a go at my own life. I was tired of always assuming that everyone but myself possessed secret information; like some common code of understanding, some idea that tethered their soul and enabled them to get through life with some degree of grace, as opposed to the panic-ridden, angry, tumbling down the pipe that I had experienced.

I really believed that when I rolled into Hollywood a welcoming committee of producers and directors would be there to greet me. They'd flag down my car and say, "Are you Marc Maron? We've been waiting for you. Hey, everyone, gather around! Marc Maron is here. Your Grandma Goldy called ahead and said you wanted to be in the movies. Is that true, kid? Well, it's your lucky day. We've begun production. There's your trailer. The script's inside. If you want to make any changes, feel free and take your time. Oh, and Marc, there's a bowl of dietetic coffee candy in the cabinet above the sink. Who loves you, baby? We'll see you on set!"

Strangely, that didn't happen. Instead, I hooked up with a friend and spent two months on his couch in Culver City. We were working on a screenplay. I think that's what it was. There doesn't seem to be any evidence of it on paper.

I also auditioned at The Comedy Store on Sunset Boulevard and I got the job as a doorman. You had to be a comic to be a doorman and vice versa. Within a month I became head doorman.

If you don't already know it, The Comedy Store is a dark temple of fear and pain that to this day I believe is built over one of the existing gates to Hell. Evil emanates up through the floors of the place and passes into the souls of all who work there. The good ones make it funny. I was thrilled to have that opportunity.

My first night at work I became enchanted. I felt like a part of me was home. Somewhere in my soul I knew the place. I could feel what had gone on there. The current that crackled in the air of The Comedy Store was the sentient residue of an arcane period of old Hollywood indulgence. The ghosts of dark fun occupied every inch of the place, and they welcomed me like a friend who had been lost.

The structure's first incarnation was called the Clover Club. It was a drinking joint and illegal gambling parlor that was frequented by David O. Selznick and Harry Cohn. The vice squad shut it down in the late thirties. The most significant occupant of the building (besides the Devil who was always there) was Ciro's. It opened in 1940 and it was the hottest club on the strip. Sinatra, Nat King Cole, Marlene Dietrich, Billie Holiday, Martin and Lewis and Mae West all performed there. After recovering from his car wreck, a pre–Satan-worshiping Sammy Davis, Jr., debuted his new glass eye in a comeback performance at Ciro's. All of Hollywood's royalty partied there: Bogart, Gable, and Cooper. There were rumors that both a murder and an abortion had taken place in a back room of the club and that the ghost of one, the other, or both was always floating about. There were also rumors of black magic and ritualistic sex. It was where what lurked behind the black and white stills I was obsessed with in my youth would come out and cut loose. Ciro's closed in 1957.

The building lay dormant until a maternal Jewish succubus named Mitzi Shore joined forces with the Devil in a philanthropic joint venture and opened The Comedy Store in 1970. The Comedy Store is the Devil's way of giving back to the world. He understands the pain of being alienated for being a smart-ass. He wanted to give others the opportunity to try to make it work for them. Through Mitzi, he provided a venue for that purpose.

The entire outside of the club was painted black and covered with names written in cursive in white paint. These were the names of the comics who had performed at the Store regularly throughout its history. It was like a goofy rendition of the Vietnam War Memorial in Washington, D.C., only the names on the walls of the Store had died a different kind of death, and it could be repeated anytime they'd get on stage. There was also a patio bar in front of the club, facing Sunset Boulevard. It was usually occupied by a huddle of comics waiting to go on and hangers-on waiting to get off.

The inside of the club was labyrinthine and done in a red and black theme with no other variations. There were three performance rooms with different seating capacities. I lifted the velvet rope in all of them at one point or another. The largest, called the Main Room, was a Vegas-style showroom with high ceilings and a large red stage with black curtains. The Original Room was smaller, box-like and black. Audience members were seated right up to the lip of the stage. This is the classic comedy club setup. The Belly Room was upstairs. It was a small red venue used for special shows. There were hidden rooms behind all of the stages, stairways, a kitchen, lighting booths, cubbyholes, and offices upstairs. The beautiful, Gothic, Deco tone of the original Ciro's was eerily maintained. There were neon caricatures of old movie stars on the walls of the Original and Main rooms. The comic on stage in the Main Room knew it was time to get off when the bow in Fanny Brice's hair lit up. In the Original Room, it was Eddie Cantor's eyes.

The hallways were lined with the headshots of the hundreds of comics that had appeared there; some known, some unknown. A headshot differs from a portrait in that a good portrait captures the stature and spirit of its subject as a testament of who he or she is in the world. A headshot is a desperate cry for attention. It's an image designed to mask the subject's need for work and love with an attitude, gesture, or look that might be marketable. Since the headshots were all of comics, the collective neediness was hard to hide, to the point that I believed the photos on the wall were feeding on and draining the emanations of the club's illustrious dark history. It was a gallery of broken dreams. They were the pictures of people who had tried to catalyze their pain into living mirrors with which audiences could reflect their own flaws back at themselves and laugh. They were the black and white images of broken hearts in the shapes of the faces of clowns.

I moved into a small Old Spanish–style mansion that sat up on the hill behind The Comedy Store. It was called Cresthill. Mitzi owned it and rented it out to comics. It had a dark vibe as well; not as insidious as the club, but Raymond Burr had once lived there, so it possessed its own unique weird residue. There were five bedrooms, all occupied by comics. There was a full kitchen that no one ever used. There was a gas-powered fireplace in the den. I lived in a small green room with its own bathroom that had once been occupied by Andrew Dice Clay. I had no furniture other than a futon on the floor. My clothes, books, notepads, and guitars were scattered around my bed. It looked like the nest of a large animal that scavenged for building materials at a college. There was nothing on the walls except a framed still of the cast of Tod Browning's *Freaks*, which I had procured at a movie paraphernalia store in Hollywood. It hung over my bed.

Off the back of the house was a large balcony patio that was perched high over the club and looked out over the city. On mornings after long, sleepless nights of partying, some of us would piss over the balcony as the sun rose through the haze above Los Angeles. It was a glorious declaration of that strange feeling of victory that comes after surviving a night of indulgent insanity.

From here on in the story, I will be referring to the drug cocaine as "magic powder." I don't want you to judge me. I don't want you saying, "The book was interesting, but he had a drug problem."

It wasn't a "drug problem." It was the research and rituals of the religion of my choice. I was a high-level Beat adept doing deep inner-space exploration. I was journeying to the outer regions of the soul, out there where *wrong* lives.

At The Comedy Store I met many people with the magic powder. These weren't the young, shiny, upper-middle-class white kids I knew in college. No. All I'm saying is that when you're doing a lot of magic powder, generally you're not hanging out with *winners*. My new friends were the dignitaries of Hollywood's underbelly:

Satanists, porn stars, hustlers, pirates—*actual* pirates—wannabes of all kinds, washed-up child actors, drug dealers, bikers, rock stars, and evil Buddhas. Sam Kinison was the reigning king of comedy at the time. I looked up to him (I always pick the wrong Daddy figures). This wasn't a Bohemian crew. It was more like a coven of witches, or maybe the Manson family.

The first time I met Sam Kinison was at the club. I had seen him on television, but I didn't think he was that funny. Sam had heard that I was a potential initiate from his friend Carl, who I had met days before. Carl told me that he and Sam had both been doormen at the Store. Carl took a liking to me when we met, and took off his watch and gave it to me as a gift, an offering, an invitation. When I met Sam, he knew I needed to be tested. We went back to Cresthill and went one-on-one for hours. I pulled the framed photograph of the cast of *Freaks* off my wall and Sam pulled an eight ball out of his pocket. He poured the magic powder out onto the glass that covered the image of the likes of Zip the Pinhead and Johnny Eck, the legless wonder. We sat at the large dining room table with a bottle of vodka, and Sam told me the history of Sam. He had intensely focused, beady eyes. At any point during the conversation, if he thought my attention was drifting he would say, "Look me in the eyes, Maron. I like a man who can look me in the eyes."

Sam fancied himself a combination of Jesus, Elvis, and Satan. They were his heroes. He was a lapsed Baptist preacher with a bone to pick with God. He thought of himself as the *Beast*. You really had to see him live to get the full effect. He had the charisma and momentum of a human meteor. He was the comedic equivalent of pure rock 'n' roll. He elevated the frustrated suffering of the brokenhearted mortal man to anarchic hilarity. He could push an audience over the edge of their own moral parameters, throw them a line, pull them back, then push them farther off the second time. This was the technique that most interested me. It was the reason I became an aspiring adept in the Sam school. I wanted to hone the antisocial part of my personality into a craft that could earn me a living.

After about five hours of looking Sam in the eyes and listening to his bullshit, there was a lull in the conversation. So, he pulled a wad of cash out of his pocket and asked, "You ever burned money, Maron?"

"No," I said.

Sam gave me a one-hundred-dollar bill, took one for himself, and said, "Spark them up. This is great." I set the two bills on fire and Sam and I watched them burn until we couldn't hold them.

"Feels great doesn't it?" he said.

It did feel great, but that might've been because it was *his* money.

About 4:00 A.M. we ran out of magic powder, and of course we needed more. We got into my car and drove through the Hollywood night. Sam was going in and out of consciousness as he gave me directions. At one point he bolted up in his seat and said, "I don't even know you, Maron. You could kill me."

In retrospect, he was much more likely to do that to himself.

We arrived at a modern apartment building in Crescent Heights. Sam rang the bell. After a few minutes of ringing, a groggy voice was emitted from the intercom. "What? Who is it?"

"It's me," Sam said. "Let us up."

"Who's us?" the voice asked.

"Me and this kid Maron," Sam said. "He's alright."

The door buzzed.

We took the elevator up and walked down a hall, and Sam knocked on a door. It opened and there was a guy in a bathrobe standing in the doorway. He looked normal, long blond hair, mustache, wiping sleep out of his eyes.

"What the fuck? It's four-thirty," he said.

Sam barged in through the door and I followed him.

"Rick, this is Maron," Sam said. "He's the new door-man at the Store."

"Hey," Rick said.

"Hey," I said apologetically.

I later found out that Rick was a hairdresser during the day.

"You got anything?" Sam asked as he started rummaging through the kitchen like an obsessed troll.

"Yeah," Rick said. "You guys are insane."

"Any booze around?" Sam asked, opening cabinets.

"Just come into my bedroom. Be cool. I don't want to wake up my roommate."

We went into his bedroom. Sam sat down on the floor and started passing out. I stood. Rick walked into his bathroom and came back out holding two Smirnoff miniatures. He gave them to Sam.

"Here. This is all I have. I stole them off the plane."

Sam poured them, one after the other, into his mouth. He didn't do it like someone drinking. He shot them down his throat like Orson Welles did in *Touch of Evil*. It was a dull, passive motion, a necessity, fuel for a dying machine. Then Sam went out cold.

It was an awkward moment, standing there in a

stranger's bedroom over the motionless, still breathing body of the biggest star in comedy, who I barely knew and who Rick knew well and sold drugs to. I assumed he would just crash there.

"I guess I better split," I said.

"Fuck no!" Rick said. "You gotta get him out of here. I don't want him to pull a Belushi on me."

Rick handed me a bindle of magic powder, and we lifted Sam up and into consciousness and walked him out the door. I was holding Sam up in the hallway.

"He'll pay me later," Rick said. "Nice meeting you, Maron."

"Yeah, you too," I said.

Then Rick shut the door.

I got Sam back into my car. I didn't know what to do with him. I didn't know where he lived. We drove back up to Cresthill. I walked him into the house and he made his way to the den, where he lay facedown on the floor in front of the fireplace and fell immediately asleep.

I sat down at the table and poured some magic powder onto the Freaks, did a couple of lines, and went into my room. I hung the picture back up over my bed, lay down, and listened to my heart pound. I tried to assess where I was, what had happened, and my new friends as I waited to die.

Monday nights were "no cover nights" at the club, and they usually lasted until Wednesday morning. It was Sam's night. The dregs of Hollywood would pack The Comedy Store and wait for Sam to take the stage in the Main Room. He would usually show up at about 11:00, but you could feel him coming at 10:30. The place would become electric with anticipation. Even the pictures in the hallways looked excited. Sam filled the void between the past and the present. When he was around, the engine of the Hell-driven laugh mill fired on all pistons and the building came alive. He was the Devil's clown prince.

I eventually became part of the inner circle. Once Sam arrived, it was my job to get enough money from him to stock Cresthill for a party that could last anywhere from two hours to three days. I would go to the 7-Eleven on La Cienega and get two fifths and four pints of Jack Daniel's, a fifth of vodka, five or six packs of cigarettes, a case of beer, cranberry juice, and some O.J. I would go back to the house and put two fifths on the table and stash the pints in different places around the house for those who stayed the course. Around two o'clock Sam would show up with the magic powder and a crowd of freaks.

There were the regulars. There was Jumpstart Jimmy

Schubert and his gimp leg that he had crushed under a motorcycle. He was my only real friend. There was Todd L., known as The Todd, a heavyset Jewish guy who was sure he was heir apparent to Kinison's throne. He had very little of his own material but plenty of everyone else's. Todd had dated both Samantha Strong and Christy Canyon, the porn queens, so they were around. He broke up with Samantha because she had had sex with another guy, off screen. There was Steve K, who would wander around The Comedy Store asking people, "Was I on yet?" If the answer was "yes," he'd say, "How was I?" There was Sparky, the angry little red-haired rich kid who had no patience for any of it but still showed up. There was Carl, Sam's Red West. There was, of course, Rick the hairdresser, until he was expelled when Sam thought he was cutting the magic powder with pancake mix. There was Dave the Satanist who looked liked Christopher Walken. He had a pentagram tattooed over his heart; an eye in a pyramid—what he called "the mark of the Illuminati"—tattooed on his arm, and a "666" tattooed on his hand. He wasn't a bad guy, really, just annoying. Sam hated him. Hassan, the Arab, replaced Rick. The story was that Hassan had fought against the Israelis in the Six-Day War and then moved to America, was drafted, went to Vietnam, and then moved to Hollywood to sell drugs. Hassan had a deep, creepy charm. He never seemed flustered. He was prone to answering almost every question by saying, "It's only rock 'n' roll."

There were others that came and went, but they were mostly casualties stopping by on their way down, week-end-warrior types or half-innocent onlookers at the scene of an ongoing accident.

Physical liabilities aside, the magic powder made me feel *more* special than I already thought I was. Eventually comedy became secondary and the sacred rituals of magic powder became primary. My confidence grew into a mystical grandiosity that was fueled by sleep deprivation. I began to feel as if I had clairvoyant powers, that unseen psychic tendrils were emanating from my head and I could feel the souls of buildings and read the minds of people coming toward me. "Don't speak. I already know!" I would say to any approaching person.

I began to believe I had a divine purpose and was working for some unseen mystical force; that I had been assigned to Hollywood to understand the evil that resided there. An evil that was there before the film industry, before the Spanish missionaries. The evil had always been there. It was in the ground, waiting to be born.

I would stand out on the patio of The Comedy Store and people would walk up to me and I would say, "Have you seen the Hollywood sign?"

"Yeah," they'd say.

"But do you *get* it?" I'd scream.

That's where my head was at.

I saw Hollywood as a mystical Jewish city. It was like the anti-Jerusalem. Think about it. It was built on the same idea as the real Jerusalem. A small group of Jewish kings went into the desert with a crew of crack Jewish writers and created the kabala of the American myth. The movies!

They harnessed an almost Promethean power and it illuminated a sacred sequence of celluloid images run at a specific speed to generate an illusion and people would *pay money* to judge themselves against that illusion.

That's a religious idea.

Then they built a factory to mass-produce the illusion. That factory became Hollywood. To this day, passionate, talented, charismatic, but very stupid young people fuel that factory. They go to Hollywood in hordes to try to become the mythic occupants of the illusion. Myself included. This machine, this factory, creates an exhaust that hangs over Los Angeles. That's not smog. It's vaporized disappointment. It's like oxygen for the demons that live there.

I couldn't share my insights because I saw myself as a mystic spy behind enemy lines and I believed Sam was onto me. He was getting annoyed. I kept saying things like "Tell me about the dark side, man."

There was very little downtime between parties. I began hoping Sam would clutch his chest and fall face-down onto the cast of *Freaks*. I needed some sleep. Call me Judas. One Monday night the recurring Last Supper was under way. Some of the regulars were there, and sitting beside me was an incredibly drunken unidentified female object who had drifted in with one of Sam's gypsy entourages that had come and gone. She was nodding off and babbling, "I've got to be in court tomorrow."

"Why?" I said.

"Drunk driving homicide," she said, her head falling back. I looked down and noticed that one of her wrists was bandaged.

"What happened to your wrist?" I asked.

"I tried to kill myself," the woman said.

"Why didn't you do the other wrist?" I asked.

"Because I didn't want to fuck up my watch."

Then she passed out on the table and someone dragged her into Todd's room. The party kept on. Sam got up from the table and disappeared for a while, then came back. Sparky had been out checking around the house, making sure nothing was amiss. He walked up to me and whispered in my ear, "I think the Beast did something weird."

"What are you talking about?" I said.

"I think he pissed all over that girl on Todd's bed," Sparky said.

He had. It was getting too sick, too dark, and too weird. Sam was out of control. My conscience was deteriorating. The branded door in my mind had creaked open and the Gray was turning to black. I had the ominous feeling that someone was going to die and it might be me.

Then the voices started to come. The membrane that surrounds my brain had become some kind of receiver of mystical transmissions. I'm sure you've all heard of people who hear voices in their head, but I'm here to tell you that when you do, it's never one; it's always many, and you spend a lot of time trying to get them to pick a leader. "If someone's got something to say step to the front of the head."

I was standing out on the patio of The Comedy Store one night and I came to believe that the St. James Hotel, catty-corner to The Comedy Store, was transmitting the voices. The St. James Hotel is now the Argyle, but it was originally the Sunset Tower apartment building. Built in

1929, it was one of the first high-rises on the Sunset Strip. The likes of Jean Harlow, John Wayne, ZaSu Pitts, Howard Hughes, Joseph Schenk, Marilyn Monroe, and Bugsy Siegel had residences there at one time or another. It was a Deco monolith that has looked over Hollywood since the beginning. It had overseen all that had gone on. It saw Peg Entwhistle leap to her death off the "H" in the HOLLYWOOD sign in 1932. It watched Charlie Chaplin's dwarf-like physique grunt and twitch atop another teenage girl. It saw Elizabeth Short, "The Black Dahlia," her body severed, in half, left in a vacant lot in 1947. It heard Lenny Bruce's face smack down on the tiles in 1966. It watched as members of the Manson family drove up through the hills to Sharon Tate's home in the summer of 1969. It heard John Belushi's last breath and watched his soul drift up and out of Bungalow 3 at the Chateau Marmont in 1982. It watched Andy Dick drive his car into a telephone pole in 1999. When I was there it was being renovated and it was completely gutted. I thought it was providing a nesting place for the lost souls of Hollywood's Golden Era and I was picking up their chatter. They needed me. I thought perhaps they wanted me to destroy The Comedy Store so the gate to Hell would be open and they could return home.

There is a Grecian altar on top of the building. It sits

up there now. You might think, *Yeah, so? It was a decorative decision by an architect.*

Think what you want, but I believed that the end of the world was to begin on that altar.

I even knew how it was going to go down. I believed that Michael Jackson was going to drag the sacred red heifer from the Old Testament up the back stairs of the St. James Hotel—you *know* he has the animal. He'd lay the calf on the altar, put on a very special glove, raise a gold, jewel-encrusted dagger over his head, and plunge it into the heart of the calf. Then he'd do a moonwalk and begin the hundred-year period of darkness during which the illusion wins.

Okay, maybe I was doing too much magic powder, but who's to say I'm wrong? Maybe it just hasn't happened yet. Then again, *maybe it's already happened.*

One night we had a big jam session on the back balcony of Cresthill. Sam brought all his guitars and amps over, and we set them up and played loud, hard rock 'n' roll to the city of Los Angeles until the neighbors called the cops. Sam had to perform at the club, so we locked his equipment in my room. It was a Monday so the insanity commenced. Well into day two of that Monday night, Dave the Satanist showed up and sat down at the table. Within a few hours the tension between him and

Sam built to the point that Dave leapt out of his chair and shouted at Sam, "You're not a real Satanist. I'm going to report you to Anton LaVey."

The vortex was opening as the chaos turned in on itself. Sam had been up for two days, and that was when the valve between impulse and action blew. No one was safe.

"Fuck Anton LaVey!" Sam said.

Sam threw a drink in Dave's face and smacked him. This was Sam's cowardly method of hand-to-hand combat. I'd seen him do it before. A small scrape ensued, and Dave's shirt was ripped open, revealing the pentagram on his chest.

"Get the fuck out of here, freak," Sam said.

I told Dave that he should get out of the house, but he wouldn't leave. He was all shook up. I felt bad for him. I had to go meet my friend Bill, who was coming to Los Angeles for the first time. I didn't want to deal with the dueling Satanists. I locked Dave in my room so things could settle down. I split to see my friend at his hotel. I wound up crashing in his room. I needed the break. I forgot about Dave.

The next morning at around eleven o'clock my friend Bill and I walked into Cresthill. We went to my room. The door had been kicked in and all the music equipment was gone. Dave was gone. I couldn't even imagine what had transpired. There was no blood, which was good. We walked into the dining room, where Sam and a few others were still sitting at the table. I said, "What the fuck?"

Sam looked at the other people at the table and then looked at me as if he'd been waiting hours to say what he had to say. He screamed, "I pissed on your bed, Maron. You want to know why?"

"Why, Sam?" I said, surprisingly not surprised.

"Because you let that freak sleep in there with my guitars."

There was a moment of awkward silence. I turned to my friend Bill and said, "I told you I knew him."

That was the end of my training. I could no longer sleep in my bed because the Beast had peed on it. They were onto me. I had been expelled from the cabal. My paranoia became amplified to a mystical level. I saw everything as a sign connoting a grand conspiracy. I was sure that the evil forces of the universe were now after me in a very intimate and personal way. I had to try to evade them at every turn. I was living in a comic book, but I had no special powers.

I took a walk down Hollywood Boulevard the next day to assess and integrate my experiences into a life that was rapidly getting away from me. I was looking at the stars in the sidewalk, trying to find a place for their shape and meaning in my elaborate and always unfolding mythos. I cut down the side street where my car was parked. I walked by a small storefront mission church that was half filled with derelicts being preached to by a manic little man with a microphone. Two doors down from the church there was a magic store. Not the kind of magic store with fake doo-doo and coin tricks. It was the kind with candles and amulets. I hadn't really investigated or practiced Black magic in any organized fashion, so I thought that maybe it was time. I went in to browse. I needed tools.

There was a counter at the back of the store, facing the door. Behind the counter were shelves filled with jars of herbs. In the display part of the counter there were crystals, trinkets, and the ceremonial hardware of ritual. The smell of incense permeated the air. I was the only person in the place besides the two trolls that were perched behind the counter on separate stools. They had shaggy long hair and blank expressions on their faces.

There were shelves of books throughout the store. I had never seen those books or heard of the authors before. I pulled Aleister Crowley's *The Book of Lies* off the shelf and randomly popped it open to a poem numbered

23 in some kind of series. It was called "Skidoo." I read aloud to myself.

> *What man is at ease in his Inn?*
> *Get out.*
> *Wide is the world and cold.*
> *Get out.*
> *Thou has become an in-itiate.*
> *Get out.*
> *But thou canst not get out by the way thou camest in. The*
>   *Way out is THE WAY.*
> *Get out.*
> *For OUT is Love and Wisdom and Power.*
> *Get OUT.*
> *If thou hast T already, first get UT*
> *Then get O.*
> *And so at last get OUT.*

I had no idea what it meant in the context of the book, but there are no coincidences. I felt like I was in the eye of a storm and deliverance was upon me. The store was swirling with the momentum of my thoughts. Then, almost as if I had conjured it, the door blew open and a man lurched into the store. He was a very tall person. He had flaming red hair and a frenetically baffled energy about him. His gangling arms were folded tightly over his chest, as if he were trying to stop himself from exploding. His voiced wavered in volume when he spoke. "Hey, wow, this is a really great store. I had no idea it was here. How long has it been here?"

The trolls behind the counter remained expressionless.

It felt like that moment when a film sticks in the projector—that split second before the image burns up from the middle.

A folded American flag slipped out from under the man's shirt. He grabbed it, retucked it away, and pressed it to himself with his arms.

One of the trolls eased forward on his stool and said, "Why do you have an American flag folded up under your shirt?"

The man, tripping over his words in discomfort said, "It, uh, m-m-m-makes me f-f-f-feel, uh, safe."

The troll pulled his hair back over his ears, widened his eyes, and focused a gaze on the man that could radiate through walls.

"You're acting too weird," he said. "Please leave now."

"Ah, we-we-well, okay." The man seemed to melt into himself and crackle upon hearing this, and he sheepishly lurched back out the door, holding himself tightly.

The film regrooved itself. I walked up to the counter

and looked in the display case. The speaking troll was eyeing me passively.

"Hey, let's be honest here," I said halfheartedly. "What's the validity of all this magic stuff, *really*?"

He looked at me with the earnestness of a rock and said, "You don't want to open any doors you can't close."

I felt all my fears congeal around this statement. That was it. I had my special power. I would be the opener and closer of doors. I mean, I was the head doorman. A doorman of the head.

"Thanks," I said to the troll, holding eye contact long enough to get a magical jolt from his intensity. "Don't open any doors I can't close."

I felt empowered as I walked out into the half-hardened gelatin air of the Hollywood day.

That night I performed the magic powder ritual myself and went down to The Comedy Store. The cabal was there and they were ostracizing me. I was panicky. I felt as if I had no friends anymore. I walked out into the parking lot where Jumpstart Jimmy tried to comfort me. He said, "You just fucked up, man. It'll be alright in a couple of days."

I was coming unglued.

"No, you fucked up," I screamed. "You're one of them. I was *never* one of them. I came here to understand and

learn. To see! You're just a pawn of the illusion. You believe that Sam's the Beast. He's not. He's just another
fucking fat bully spreading hate around. You're all just
sheep on a dead-end path. Fuck you."

I slammed the glass I was drinking from down onto
the asphalt, and it shattered all over the parking lot.

Jimmy went back into the club as Hassan drove up in
a red convertible. I walked over to him as he was getting
out of the car. I was a bit tweaked out, wired, and scared.

"Hey, Hassan," I said. "Can I talk to you for a second?"

"What can I do for you, Marc?" he said.

"What should I do? Things are all fucked up."

In *his* eyes lay the *real* Beast. He looked at me with that
cool thousand-yard stare, smiled, and said, "You should
go do your own thing. You should *get out.*"

23 Skidoo.

"Yeah, you're right," I said. "Thanks."

Hassan started to walk toward the back door of The
Comedy Store. He turned around and shouted, "It's only
rock 'n' roll!" as he disappeared through the door into the
black and red darkness, his home in Hollywood for the
last seventy years.

When the drug dealer tells you to leave, it's *really* time
to leave.

At about 3:00 A.M. I was alone in my closet, where I

spent a lot of time during the last days of my stay in L.A. The hangers kept the voices at bay and my bed had been branded.

As some of you know, the first few hours of magic powder are great, but the following eight to twenty can be a little trying. My heart was pounding itself out of my chest. My lungs were struggling to keep themselves fueled with oxygen. I was sweating and scared.

"I don't want to die. I don't want to die. Please slow down. Don't die," I said to the darkness. Words were falling and ricocheting around my mind. Images were falling and flashing behind my eyelids like white noise.

The pristine surface of a gray steel slab appeared and faded into a perspective point far off in my mental landscape. I was on a conveyor, moving like a car on the incline of a roller-coaster. Then came the drop-off. It was like the bad part of the boat ride in *Willy Wonka and the Chocolate Factory*, overaccelerated, faces, fragments of scenes, Belushi walking toward me, light for eyes.

"Hey, John. What the fuck happened to your eyes?"

Lenny Bruce flying.

I don't want to die.

Fatty Arbuckle as a dirigible floating in the air.

I don't want to die.

The cast of *Freaks* dancing down the slab toward me at

silent-film speed, singing, "One of us, one of us, one of us."

I don't want to die.

Hassan laughing, pentagrams spinning into the stars on Hollywood Boulevard, Sam turning into a dog and pissing all over space.

No, no, fuck, no. I don't want to be at this party. Fuck. How far out can I go?

Then, in my right ear, a voice that was as clear as a bell loudly said, "You've gone far enough."

Then the ride stopped. My heart stopped in a flash of white. I gasped the gasp of a drowning man who had just surfaced and sucked life back into his lungs.

It was the voice of God. God was reaching out to me.

That was the moment my Jerusalem Syndrome became proactive.

The following day I packed everything I had into my car and whatever didn't fit I gave to Steve K. I went by Rick's and evened up with him and I picked up an eight ball for the trip. I hadn't slept in what seemed like weeks. I left Hollywood on instructions from God. I was heading to the desert with no plan other than to *Get Out.*

As I drove, the sun was beating down and my eyes were squinting. Just outside of Palm Springs I saw the wreckage of the worst car accident I had ever seen. There were cops, ambulances, fire trucks, and covered bodies all over the highway. I saw it as a sign to pull off. I checked into a hotel and waited for more instructions from God. They were not forthcoming.

That was a long couple of days at the Motel Six in Palm Springs. I walked through the streets thinking I was invisible. It was okay, though. Palm Springs is a fine place to be invisible. That's sort of what it's for. Besides, I had doors to close.

8

WHEN I arrived in Albuquerque, I didn't tell anyone I was there. I went and had photos taken
and renewed my passport. I had the feeling I might need
to leave the country on very short notice. It felt like the
world was closing in on me or, at the very least, following me around. It was as if day-to-day reality was a sham
and everyone involved in it who saw me knew I was onto
them. I believed that I could move things with my mind,
that I could tell if people were evil by looking in their
eyes, and most of them were.

I stayed with my parents, who, surprisingly, weren't
evil. I tried to give them the impression that everything
was fine and I was just taking a little break. I spent a
month at home. I got clean, I bought some cowboy
boots, and I had a brief affair with a witch.

I went by The Living Batch to see if Gus was evil and I came across Robert Anton Wilson and Robert Shea's *The Illuminatus! Trilogy*. On the cover was the eye in the pyramid, the mark of the Illuminati. I brought the book up to the counter and Gus said, "Why waste your time with such utter bullshit?"

I thought he might be one of them.

I bought the book and read it cover to cover. It is a convoluted, satirical novel about magical and political secret societies, the primary one being the Illuminati, and their manifest destiny of controlling the world and the minds of its occupants on all levels. I read the book with no sense of its irony. I believed it and saw it as my Bible, a primer for productive paranoia. There was definitely an evil conspiracy at hand. It had roots in ancient Egypt, Bavaria, and perhaps the lost city of Atlantis. Aliens might have been involved at some point, but that's really conjecture. The conspiracy had moved through the people and institutions that have controlled the world for centuries. I decided it was my duty to seek it out in reality and present it to the world. It was what God wanted. I could begin to label the signs and hang them on the doors. This would be my secret mission. I moved back to Boston to restart my comedy career, a perfect cover.

When I got back east, I got a job pulling espresso at a

pre-Starbucks coffee shop in Harvard Square. It was a haven for young, confused, aspiring everythings. Faux Bohemians dressed in vintage clothes. If they couldn't find integrity in their own time, maybe they could find it in the pants of another time. I was the paranoid, bitter guy working the steamer, talking about himself. "I used to hang out with Kinison. I am an outlaw visionary. I can see the future." A *whoosh* of steam would cloud my face as I pulled the nozzle out of the frothy milk and poured it into the coffee. "You want shaved chocolate or cinnamon on this?"

I got a room in the attic of a large house in Somerville, a working-class town next to Cambridge. It was one of those group houses that people who had no idea what they were going to do with their lives passed through on their way to themselves. The room I rented was entirely covered in sky-blue paint. There are no coincidences. Within days of moving in I did some research on the color blue's mystical connotations in a book on colorology. "Blue is the color of depth, spiritual searching, serenity, change, and moon issues." Four out of five ain't bad. I was anything but serene, and I was willing to deal with my moon issues as soon as I figured out what the fuck they were.

I was given a series of dates to do stand-up in a basement in Allston at a club called Play It Again Sams. The old-movie theme didn't elude me. The coincidences were coming down like hail. Two Tuesdays a month for six months opening for an X-rated hypnotist who could make people act like strippers or dogs.

At home I put in the research. I bought the literature of the hard-core conspiracy theorists. *The Unseen Hand* and *The New World Order* by Ralph Epperson, the first edition of *Apocalypse Culture* edited by Parfrey out of Amok Press in Los Angeles, and, of course, the daily newspapers.

The thing about conspiracy literature is that it's perfect for stupid people who want to seem smart and ground their hatred in something completely mystical and confusing, and it's good for smart people who are too lazy to do their homework. People can't argue with it without possibly implicating themselves.

Facts play only a minor role in any conspiracy theory. The proximity of one series of facts to an event that might connect those facts to another series of facts is what it's really about. The object of the game is to connect the disparate facts in any way possible to get the outcome of "We're fucked." Events can be broad, shady, real, unreal, preferably convoluted, and hard to deconstruct in any one way. This leaves them open to endless possible interpretations. An event can be broken down in many ways—as long as it serves as a doorway to the facts that you want to connect. An event can revolve around a person involved, a color, a time, a government, a number, a date, a code, a logo, a distant relative, a passing moment at a point in time other than the time of the event, a bullet, an institution, forces of nature that are suspect in their timing, a sexual encounter, a coworker, or basically anything that will enable you to construct your own arcane projectile riff that you can ride to your version of the truth. That's really a matter of style.

Within a few weeks my room looked like the Son of Sam's apartment. There were holes in the walls, writing on the ceiling; books were strewn about and charts were pinned up. I was diagramming something. I was connecting the dots of the grand puzzle. One incident that I recall occurred over morning coffee. I had bought the *Boston Globe* and on the front page was a picture of then President George Bush. I cut it out and pinned it on the wall.

Bush, of course, was the vice president under Reagan and the ex–head of the National Republican Committee, the CIA, and Eli Lilly and Co. He was a member of the Skull and Bones club at Yale and probably performed their secret mock-death ritual during which the participants lie in a coffin, blindfolded, and share their sexual history with the other members. He belonged to the Freemasons and the Trilateral Commission. He was involved with the Bay of Pigs and the Iran-Contra affair. The image in the paper was of Bush attending a Texas Longhorns game. Both his hands were up in the air, his thumbs holding down his two middle fingers, thus forming a two-fisted Satan sign popular with heavy metal fans. So, of course, I thought, *How clear does it have to be? He's the Devil. The illuminated one. The bringer of light. A thousand points of light!*

I dismissed the fact that it was also the hand sign of the Texas Longhorns. Does it really matter? A cow, Satan; signs are signs. They are open to interpretation.

I called the *Boston Globe* and asked them what it would take to get a copy of the picture. The woman on the phone told me it would be $250 and asked me what I'd be using the photograph for and I said, "Evidence."

She said, "What does that mean?"

That was the end of the conversation. I hung up. I wasn't ready to get into it with the press.

I *was* ready to go to Washington, D.C. Jim, my Beatnik brother from college, was there. The Vietnam War obsession usually leads to some sort of engagement with the political charade. He had worked on the ad-

vance team for the Dukakis campaign and was freelanc-
ing in Washington. I thought Jim might've gotten himself in over his head. I was worried about what he didn't
know. I had to go see if he was okay. I needed to explain
to him what was really going on in the nation's capital.

I got on the road to Washington and tried to plan what
I would say. When I got there, I immediately called Jim.

"Jim, it's Marc. What's up, man? You okay?"

"Marc!" He was excited. "What's up? Where have you
been? What are you up to, man?"

"Jim, I need to talk to you about some stuff."

"What? What's going on? Are you alright?" He was
concerned.

"I'm fine. Are you alright?" I probed.

"Yeah, I'm great, really great. I love doing advance."

"Yeah, that's what I'm worried about." I was saddened
by the idea that I might be too late.

"What?"

"Well, I don't think we should talk about it over the
phone. We need to meet in person."

"Umm, alright."

"It really couldn't be more important."

"Well, I'm not going to be up there for—" I cut him off.

"I'm here, man. I'm in Washington."

"You're here? Great, swing by."

"No, I really can't do that, not now. Pick a place and I'll meet you."

An hour later we met on the mall in front of the Washington Monument. I gave my old friend a hug. I started to feel Jim out a bit as we walked.

"This place has a weird energy to it," I said. "It's bigger than I thought it was."

"That's right, I forgot," Jim said. "You've never been here. I'll give you the tour. It'll be great."

"It's got a *really* weird energy to it," I said. "It's the way it's built. You know about that, right?"

"What, the monument?" he asked.

"Yeah, the monument is on a grid with the Capitol that's separated by the reflecting pool. It's based on an ancient ritual plan from Atlantis. As long as this stays intact, they'll have control of the world, now that the implementation of television was successful," I said like a scientist.

Jim laughed. "Yeah, it's all a big evil thing, Marc." He was being sarcastic. He thought I was joking.

"I think we're all in trouble with Bush."

"Yeah, well, he won," Jim said. "He won't be there forever."

"He's a Trilateralist, you know?" I said. "He kisses

Bilderberger ass and does the monkey dance for the insiders at the Bohemian club."

"Yeah," Jim said and laughed. "You're not one of those
people now, are you?" Jim asked.

"What kind of people are you talking about? What
kind of person are *you* now, Jim? Hey, do you think we
can go to the Illuminati office while we're here? I'd like to
take a tour of that place."

Jim gave me a puzzled look and ignored the question.
I pulled back for a while. We toured the city and Jim
pointed out the sights, but everything started to come together and break apart simultaneously as we walked
around the rotunda of the Capitol.

I said, "Come on, man, are we going to walk around
office buildings all day?"

Jim was honestly shocked and said, "This isn't an office building. This is the Capitol of the United States of
America."

We were standing in front of busts of the founding fathers and dead senators, silly haircuts captured in stone
and I lunged. "Jim, do you understand what's going on
here? These guys?" I said, pointing at the statues behind
me. "These guys were a cabal of renegade deist freaks.
They used to have ritual circle jerks, kill goats, wear the

silly hats and chant incantations. That's why they all left England. Because they couldn't practice Satanism. Then they came here and built a government based on it. I mean, come on, the Pentagon! Pen-ta-gon. The Military Industrial Complex is in the business of round-the-clock human sacrifice with the U.N. security force. Wake up, my friend. Listen to me, I know."

"What are you talking about?" Jim said. "The founding fathers had nothing to do with the Pentagon. It was built much later."

"Yeah, but it's *all* built on the great secret keepers' original mystical momentum," I said confidently.

"What *momentum?*"

"The founding fathers knew it. They rode the momentum. They were all out of control. How could they not be? Think about it, Jim. After the Revolutionary War, when all the leftover soldiers and mercenaries went up into the hills to fuck Indians and create hillbillies, these guys had all the land. They were partying because they knew they would run the world. Ben Franklin was a freak! Every other day he'd send his boy out. Picture it, Jimmy."

I pulled my glasses down to the end of my nose like Ben Franklin.

"I want you to go over to George Washington's place

and pick up some reefer. Tell him you want the good shit and not the kind he makes rope from. Tell him Benny sent you and he'll set you up with a nice bag. Then stop by Tommy Jefferson's. If he's coming, tell him to bring the black chicks. Hurry now. If you get back here before the party, I'll hook you up to the kite again. You'd like that, wouldn't you, Toby? Now go, score, Godspeed."

"Come on, Marc. That just isn't true," Jim said.

"You come on, man. They were all Masons, all of them. Dirty, dark Freemason spin-offs of Weishapt's Order of the Illuminati. Ben Franklin was an old-school Hellfire Club kinky Mason. Jesus, Jim, you want me to pull a dollar bill out of my pocket and show you?! The fucking eye in the pyramid is the mark of the Illuminati. Get it? FDR put it on the dollar. Roosevelt was Mr. New Deal modern Mason, ushering in the one-world government, opening the door for Trilateralism. You gotta listen to me, man. It's true. I read this in a book written by a guy who writes books."

"I don't think you really understand how politics works," Jim said dismissively.

"So what?" I yelled. "Is that what this is really about? Politics?"

"No, Marc. Why don't you tell me what it's all about?" he said, trying to provoke and placate me simultaneously.

"Wake up and feel the momentum, Jimmy! It pacifies the masses with entertaining psychic terrorism delivered by the media industrial complex until no one knows what's real or who they are anymore. They go on thinking they know, but they are unable to care about anything. It leaves them walking through life as controllable husks in search of their souls, with ghost limbs for hearts to guide them. Then Big Business and the big banks sell them back to themselves piecemeal in the form of products and designed ways of life. Then the excited husks will begin to feel as though they are whole again, but they will only regain as much as they can afford to buy back, yet still be in debt. That's the core of it. The hope of getting all of themselves back keeps control intact and self-actualization nearly impossible. That's what democracy is protecting now, Jim, hungry fear. That is the American way. That is the pursuit of happiness. The President of the United States is just the highest level of middle management. This government is just placating the people and keeping them lost so the insiders—their families, their friends, business associates—can feed. It's the momentum, man!" I smiled, knowingly.

"You might have pushed yourself out too far this time. Are you on something, or are you nuts, Marc?" Jim said. I scream-whispered.

"Bush is a Freemason! That's why Dukakis didn't win. He's not in on it! You should know that. It all funnels through Washington, Jim! The atomic bomb, the Cold War, the Kennedy assassination, the CIA, the Vietnam War, Watergate, Iran-Contra, have shattered the people's belief in any truth when it comes to their part in the political process. That's part of the grand plan: All truth becomes manifest when there's nothing anyone can do about it. How clear does it have to be?" I yelled. "This city is the momentum's mystical switchboard for the hundred-year period of darkness, and I think you've seen the controls. Have you? Own it, man. Tell me I'm lying."

I'm out of breath. I'm not even sure what I've just said. People are staring. Jim just looks at me and says, "Marc, listen to me. People here just aren't that organized."

There was a moment of stillness, entropy. I had been hit with an arrow of truth that I just couldn't deny. I took in what he said. "They aren't?" I asked, unsure.

"No, of course not. The system works. It's the best government on the planet. There are some bad people, but it just isn't one big evil plan. Democracy doesn't allow the bad people to hang around too long. They are found out and brought down by the Senate, by the Congress, by the people. Sorry, Marc." Jim patted me on the back.

Of course, he was right. How could they possibly be

that organized? It was a ridiculous idea. I felt like I had been shaken awake from a dream. It deflated my entire cosmology. My all-encompassing, spiritual, mystical, symbolic system of evil was laid to wreckage in the rotunda of the Capitol. I didn't really know anything. I had nothing. I was lost. I was in exile. It was sad. Who was I? What channel was I on? I said good-bye to Jim and I slouched back to Boston to be reborn.

9

THE momentum had pummeled me. I was caught in the undertow. When I got back to Boston, I took all the diagrams off the wall and gave my books to a guy down the hall who I didn't like. Then I sat in my blue room and smoked cigarettes for two years. That's really all I did. Smoked, did comedy, and waited for some kind of sign. I had gotten off the path somehow. I was out of the mystical groove. The doors had all slammed shut.

I started to realize that my relationship with God was tenuous at best, but my relationship with the Philip Morris company and Marlboro cigarettes was very deep, had been for years. I started to believe that was really the core of my spirituality, American spirituality, *brand loyalty.* It requires an almost religious faith. You don't realize how strong that faith is or how deep it runs until it is tested.

My faith was tested in a convoluted way. I woke up one morning, coughed my guts out, and screamed, "What am I, an idiot?" and decided that I had to quit smoking. I believed that the only way I could quit smoking would be to go to the Philip Morris plant in Richmond, Virginia, where I would stand before the corporate machinery that went into giving me cancer. I would be moved to horror and shout in a powerful, condemning way, "This is evil! This is bad! I'm done with it." There was even the outside chance, given my power at that time, that I would actually stop the machinery with my will and lead the workers out of the factory.

I called my friend Jim, who I hadn't spoken to since the Washington episode the year before and said, "Jimmy, it's Marc. I need to quit smoking. We need to go to Virginia now."

Jim said, "Alright, man, swing by." He was in Boston at that time.

We got on the road and drove nine hours, straight from Boston to Richmond. We pulled into the parking lot of the Philip Morris plant and I have to be honest with you, it's a beautiful building. I mean really nice.

We walked into this plush lobby and welcoming area.

There was art hanging on the walls. It was very tasteful. There was some modern art, some folk art, and some classic American paintings. There was a little something for everyone. There's room for everyone under the meaty leaves of the tobacco plant. A pleasant-looking woman wearing a smart dress and glasses sat at a desk. There was a sign on that desk that I saw the minute I walked in that said PLEASE FEEL FREE TO SMOKE.

Warmth filled me. I was excited to be there. I was home.

There was a museum connected to the lobby, featuring an exhibit that charted the history of tobacco. There were dioramas showing how the settlers learned how to cultivate tobacco from the Indians and then how the settlers cultivated their own fields and then how the settlers brutally massacred the Indians, apparently as thanks for helping them.

Then there was a tour of the actual factory. I couldn't have been more thrilled. Everyone got in golf carts, three to a cart. Each cart had a brand label on the side. There was a Marlboro cart. There was a Benson & Hedges cart. I was on the Merit cart. Who the hell smokes Merits? Why didn't it just say PUSSY on the side?

So, there I was in the pussy cart, three cars back from the front, feeling like a neutered little girl. I watched angrily as the pioneering Marlboro cowboys got to view the machinery of cancerous mass production first, but I settled in and began to enjoy the tour.

We all had to wear headsets because the machinery was so loud. The woman who was giving the tour had to speak into a microphone and the only reason she would stop was to say "This machine to the right makes over a million cigarettes—*hack, hack, hack.*" It was an awful, rattling cough. To hear that sound amplified in your head if you're a smoker is oddly bonding. *It's okay, honey. We understand. Pull over and spit if you need to.*

The most amazing thing about the tour was that workers were smoking as they operated the machinery. It was beautiful. It looked like Utopia. It's what socialism was supposed to look like. What's the boss going to do? Tell them they can't smoke?

There's a doctor's office right on the premises. That's health coverage. You have to figure it's necessary. Some guy's working the machine and he screams, "Oh, the pain shooting down my arm!" He's taken to the doctor's office.

The doctor says, "You know, this is the third time this month with the angina, Bob. You gotta quit smoking."

"What are you kidding? Look where I work."

The doctor takes a long drag off his butt and responds,

"You don't gotta tell me, Tiger. I've been here for seventeen years. I'm just a little luckier than you."

After the tour we are led into what I like to call "the temple room" of the Philip Morris plant. It was a small theater where I had the corporate revelation. They had borrowed the illusion-making magic from the Jews in Hollywood to create a film presentation illuminating the mythic power of Philip Morris.

At that point in my life I understood abstract conspiracy theory and the evil momentum. I had no real concept of how corporations worked. I didn't know that corporations could own other corporations. That they all linked together to create the malignant mesh of commerce that now envelops the planet. It didn't matter. I wasn't strong enough to fight anymore.

The lights go down and the film begins. An authoritative but friendly voice blasts itself into our heads. It has a celebratory tone to it, like marching music should be playing.

"Philip Morris makes Marlboro cigarettes and many other brands enjoyed around the world . . ."

Then there's a montage of people smoking, all with different haircuts, different skin colors, different clothing—lederhosen, dark glasses; in France, Japan, the Arctic Circle; dancing, hooray, smoking around the globe . . .

"Philip Morris also owns Kraft Foods . . ."

Huh? Who knew? Kraft Foods is Oscar Mayer, Velveeta, Macaroni and Cheese, all those artery-jamming convenience foods that you cooked when you didn't know how to cook but you had to eat something.

"Philip Morris also makes Miller Beer . . ."

The worst beer in the world.

And for dessert, Philip Morris recently acquired Nabisco. Have an Oreo.

It looked like the food pyramid from Hell.

After the film we were led as new converts to the gift shop. They have a gift shop at Philip Morris where they give you a pack of cigarettes. *Give* you one.

"The first time is always free." Satan's motto.

"What if I don't smoke?"

"I bet you got a friend that does. These are fresh. Smell them. They're still warm. Feel them. You got kids? You don't have to give them to the kids. Just put them in a drawer. They'll find them."

I surrendered. The momentum won again. I chose a pack of Player Navy Cuts, an English import. I went there to quit smoking and I left smoking filterless. But I felt connected to something big, something global, something all encompassing. A community. An international congregation of vice and weakness. Love is a democratic ideal that knows no boundaries. So are cigarettes.

There are so many things in my life like that; Coca-Cola, for instance. I drank seven today. I'm drinking one as I write this. Is that a problem? Okay, so I drank two. Look at a Coke can. It's beautiful, the red and white, the letters, the "C" with the little curlicue that represents the Ourbouros, the serpent eating its own tail, which is an ancient mystical symbol of the alchemists connoting primordial undifferentiated substance and the universe's ability to regenerate itself.

Maybe I'm reading too much into it. So?

Coke is it. It's the real thing. I'd like to buy the world a Coke. That elevated feeling you get when you crack open a can of Coke and bring it to your lips and the sweet fizz runs up into your sinuses before you even taste the soda. The first sip of the perfectly carbonated nectar pops your taste buds open and then runs down your throat and warms your stomach. That feeling, that wholeness, that abandon, for a few seconds. Then, that itch, that need for another sip. It's okay, there's more. There's always more.

There was a time when we thought there might not be any more Coke. It was a sad time. It happened when I was in college. It was the great Coca-Cola panic of 1985. New Coke had hit the shelves and confusion and chaos were the rule of the day. There was the looming threat that the Coke we all knew and loved was going away for good. New Coke was bad, tasted like Pepsi. So, like many people, I began stockpiling the old Coke. I had a stack of cases in my kitchen. As they dwindled, the panic set in and I thought that the traditional Coke would be lost forever. It turned out to be a big trick to test our loyalty, control us, corral us, and show us how powerful they were. They released Coke Classic in late 1985 and everything was okay again.

I remember being in Atlanta for a gig. The Coca-Cola Museum is in Atlanta. I was beside myself. I couldn't wait to go. When I got there, I walked down a long, arched corridor that seemed to be made out of the same green glass that the old Coke bottles were made out of. At the end of the corridor was a young man sitting at an information desk. I walked to the desk and quietly said, "Is there a room for private worship? Maybe just me and the product and a mat with some old Coke jingles playing softly?"

He laughed and said, "No, there is not. We have the museum and the fountain room. Would you like a ticket?"

I said, "Yes, please. Thank you." I went into the Coca-Cola Museum.

I went to the fountain room first. It was a dark room with spotlighted self-serve soda machines all around its perimeter. There was a light show in the form of fountains running water from the ceiling that were illuminated with strobe lights, giving the effect of the water actually running upward toward Heaven. Each machine had five dispensers. They had Coca-Cola, Fanta, Sprite, Tab, Fresca, Diet Coke, Mr. Pibb, Mello Yello, Ramblin' Root Beer, Cherry Coke, and the evil, awful New Coke. There were brand names that were alien to me. That was because Coca-Cola makes and distributes many sodas that aren't available in the United States. They wouldn't suit our tastes. I tried all of them. Germany's Kinley, Sweden's Mer, the U.K.'s Lilt, and the Nordic Kuli. There was Limca, Gold Spot, Maaza from India. Japan's Calo and Shpla. Royal Tru Orange from the Philippines and the amazing-tasting lychee-flavored Tian Yu Di from China. Lychee nut soda, fucking unbelievable, the power of it all.

As I walked through the exhibits I found the most fascinating historical element of the museum was the Coca-Cola logo itself, the white cursive on the red background. How it has traveled through time from 1886 to the present. Governments have changed, fashions have changed, countries have tumbled, World Wars have been fought, and nuclear bombs detonated, but the Coca-Cola logo lives on unchanged. No force of man or nature can damage the integrity of it. That logo represents something much larger than the ebb and flow of history. It represents a powerful consistency that looms sometimes largely and sometimes subtly over all things, like God.

It is but one in the modern pantheon of new gods! Philip Morris, AT&T, GE, AOL, General Motors, Time Warner, Viacom, Microsoft: Do we have a choice? Con Ed. Is there a moment that goes unpaid for? Did you leave anything on at home? Sprint, Levi Strauss, Disney, Nike, Sony. I have a Sony VCR, a Sony CD player, a Sony Walkman, a Sony television. I mean, where would we be without Sony? Certainly unentertained. Sony: It has four letters like "good," like "love."

These corporate entities quell our fears, they give us hope, and they make us feel as if we are part of something eternal and lasting. They present us with a manufactured reality that comforts us. In essence, they do everything God used to do.

All I know is that when I'm in a spiritual crisis, I'll do

anything—smoke, eat, drink, watch TV, get online, buy something, listen to music, go to the movies, take a drive—anything but get down on my knees and say, "God, it's Marc. I don't know who I am anymore. Can you help me?"

10

YEARS went by and I had very little communication with God. I started working professionally as a comic. Doing all the clubs in the Boston area and driving hours into the New England countryside to do one-nighters in Massachusetts, New Hampshire, Rhode Island, Maine, and Vermont. The road became part of my job. The romantic idea of it dissipated.

I let go of most of my conspiratorial ideas until my first television appearance was preempted by the Gulf War. It was *An Evening at the Improv*. I did this joke on that show: "Don't you think calling George Bush the environmental president is kind of like saying, 'Well, you know Hitler *was* a vegetarian.'?" I was sure that Bush had seen it, he personally called A&E, and had them drop the show and I was put on a list.

Around this time I began seeing Kim, the woman I would eventually marry. I met her at my brother's wedding. She was the maid of honor and I was the best man. She lived in Boston, I lived in Boston. It was almost like we *had* to get married. It was predestined. After my brother's wedding I moved in with her. We came together in that perfect mixture of love and my need of a place to live. That lasted about a year.

We broke up for a while and Kim moved to San Francisco. I moved to New York and lived on the Lower East Side for a couple of years. I couldn't really integrate myself into the New York scene. I was too angry for the New York clubs and alienated audiences. I would drive up to Boston on weekends to make money. I eventually started to come unglued and packed up everything I had into my car, again, except for my futon frame. I gave that to the Realist painter across the hall who had been sleeping on his floor and I left.

I got on the road to San Francisco to see if Kim would save me. I made the trip in three and a half days. The last stint of driving was from Wyoming to San Francisco, twenty-two hours straight through. My eyes were watering and lights were trailing when I drove over the Bay Bridge up into Bernal Heights, where I collapsed on Kim's porch until she came home from work. She let me move in with her and we tried to rebuild our relationship while I tried to build a comedy career.

Within a few weeks of my being in San Francisco, my friend Stu called me from L.A. and told me Sam Kinison had been killed in a car accident. It was a head-on collision with a drunk teenager. Stu told me that Carl had been right behind him in another car and that Sam died in Carl's arms. I was horrified, relieved, and incredibly insensitive. "I don't care what middle act's arms he died in. It should've happened when people gave a shit about him. Then maybe he could've become mythic."

All I could really think about when I heard that Sam was dead was finding out where he was buried so I could go there and pee on his grave. I owed him that.

San Francisco was a great place to have coffee for a couple of years. The comedy scene was deeply rooted and the community was very supportive of its comics. I was able to do the kind of comedy I wanted to do, and it was received well. If it hadn't been for San Francisco, I probably would've spontaneously combusted.

I had been living there a year when I got a call from my manager telling me that I was wanted in New York to host a show on Comedy Central. It was called *Short Attention Span Theatre* and the producers had chosen me to drive it. I couldn't understand why. Here I was doing this angry, philosophical, rant-oriented comedy and they wanted me to host their happy little show that was on three times a day. I resisted at first, but when I looked at my nearly empty date book, I really had no choice. I took the job and eventually Kim and I moved back to New York.

Short Attention Span Theatre was a clip show. We showed clips of movies and TV shows usually organized under themes as broad as "Jews" or "the color blue." We actually did both of those themes. We could only use clips that were the property of Comedy Central or those that had been provided by companies that were releasing a movie, a video, or TV show. That way it didn't cost anything. I did a monologue and usually one sketch piece. I really hated doing the show. I thought it clipped my wings, never really allowing me to be me. I saw it as a hostage situation. I was being held paid prisoner by Viacom, the owner of Comedy Central and Time-Warner, the owner of HBO, which produced my show. Three times a day people who were home from school or worked late or just didn't have much of a life could see me being cute in borrowed clothing as I presented promotional material disguised as show substance under a stupid theme. In retrospect, it taught me how to be on television, which was good. I learned to be a part of the illusion. It also got me a reputation for being hard to work with, which was bad.

The show was supposed to be taking place in the vault of Comedy Central. Every episode opened with my side-kick, the elevator operator, and me going down to the vault in an elevator. The set was supposed to be a base-ment with shelves cluttered with reels, files, and boxes with funny labels. Right in the middle of the set there was a pyramid of twelve televisions that were turned on. It was my background. I stood in front of it every day. I was on TV, I was in the TV, and TVs that I was on sur-rounded me. I wish my Grandpa Jack had been alive to see me *really* on the TV. It was as if the series of photo-graphs I took in high school were some kind of personal prophecy.

The most significant event that occurred during my tenure as host of *SAST*, other than interviewing Lily Tomlin, happened on a press junket. I was flown by Comedy Central to Los Angeles to help announce their new season. They had booked me a room at the St. James Hotel. I couldn't believe it. I was so freaked out and ex-cited. I was going to be inside the hotel that communi-cated with me when I had lived in Hollywood years before, during what seemed like another life. I could barely contain myself when I got there. When I walked into the St. James, tingles ran through my body. All the doors started to creak open again.

The first night there, after I had done all my press conferences, I walked over to The Comedy Store. I didn't see anyone I knew, so I walked back over to the St. James. I went up into my room and lay on my bed. The décor was beautiful—delicate Deco glassware and picture frames and polished chrome fixtures in the bathroom. The furniture and the bed were 1920s reproductions. Everything about it just brought my mind back to those pictures in Irv's books; to that feeling of royalty and radiation that came off of those film stills mixed with the darkness of the hotel's past, of my past. I just took in the energy of the place. It was so important to me from the outside when I was crazy. I could still feel something.

At about twelve-thirty that night, I couldn't help myself. I was driven by a compulsion much bigger than I was. I went up the stairs to the roof door. There was no alarm, so I went out onto the roof. There was another door and a ladder that went up to the altar. *The altar.* I pulled the door open and went up the ladder. I stood beneath the altar. I looked down at Los Angeles. I looked down at the hills and The Comedy Store. It was oddly windy up there and the sky seemed to be crackling with electricity. I felt as if I were finishing a ritual that I had inadvertently started years before. I felt transcendent. I was possessed by a madness for closure. I took some deep breaths and yelled at the sky, "Where are you now?" There was no immediate response.

I went back down to my room and went to sleep. I was woken up in the middle of the night by the sound of tinkling glass. I couldn't figure out what it was at first, because I was half asleep. Then I heard another layer of sound: The building was creaking. Then I heard the muffled voices of panic, people scrambling around in the hallway, trying to figure out what to do. Beneath it all was an even deeper layer of sound, the shifting of the Earth's plates. It was the best experimental music I had ever heard, except that it was being spontaneously generated by an earthquake in progress. God was jamming— just for me. I bolted out of bed. The building was swaying back and forth. I was in my underwear and I didn't know what to do. I thought I should stand in the doorway, that's what I remember my dad saying, but I wanted out. I didn't know if I should put my pants on or not, but then I thought, *I don't want to be the only one standing outside with no pants on.* I put them on and went downstairs.

The Earth stopped rumbling after a minute or two. There were about fifteen other people in front of the hotel. I suggested that someone get his car out of the garage and bring it up so we could hear the radio broadcasts about the damage and what we should expect. We all huddled together like primitives, only it was around a Lexus so we could listen to the radio.

I pulled away and stood, looking at the blackened hills of Hollywood. There wasn't a light on anywhere, just the moonlit dark silhouette of the hills against a deep blue backdrop. This guy Jon came over and stood next to me. I had met him earlier. He was one of the producers of *Beavis and Butt-Head*. We stood there for a few quiet minutes watching the night sky light up in flashes over the valley as power stations exploded in the distance. It was eerie, and beautiful in a way. Jon looked at me pensively, and said, "I can't help but think this is somehow my fault." Maybe it was, but I was thinking the same thing about myself. He was guilty of a much more public, ritualized evil but I'd like to think that my little moment on the roof was equally as powerful in some way, maybe for the good.

In April 1997 another light flashed across the sky. After years of her putting up with my insanity, Kim and I got married. It was a traditional Jewish ceremony, hot-rodded a bit for the modern Jew palate. It was outdoors, in the dusk light of a Phoenix sunset. In the middle of our vows many guests claimed they saw a shooting star or a meteor or a UFO, but *something* went flying by.

Everyone assumed it was good luck. So we assumed it was good luck. Deep in my heart, I wasn't so sure, but I loved Kim. We'd been through a lot together.

Within seconds of getting married, the living potential great-grandparents and grandparents start their chorus: "Babies. When, when babies?" Babies are like cocaine to grandparents. The need comes from a deep place. They want one more opportunity to love something that hasn't disappointed them yet.

I started to see marriage as a capitalist conspiracy designed to keep people in bondage until they create new consumers. Think about the forces involved when you have a wedding. All the department stores are in on it. The religions of the world are all part of it. Kim's parents were like kingpins of the conspiracy. When you get married, you don't just get a spouse, you get dozens of expensive gifts from people you don't really know. Are they friends? Maybe, but probably not. Are they the dark faces of the conspiracy? Yes. They give you rugs, blenders, and flatware. I didn't even know what flatware *was* until I got married. If you know what it is, it may be too late for you. They give you these gifts in the guise of getting you started. They say things like, "This is to begin your life together. To start building your home." That's not really why they give this stuff to you. They give it to you so you don't leave each other. The conspiracy knows that at some point in the first couple of years of marriage you will have a moment of existential crisis and say, "What the fuck did I do? I don't even know you! I want out." Then you'll pause, look around, and say, "Oh, but the rug, and our blender. We make drinks in our blender. Our forks—I love our forks. I'm sorry. Right now I think I love everything here except you. That'll come and go. If it goes away for good, we can have kids and sublimate our disdain and indifference for each other in them by spoiling them and guaranteeing a legacy of misery."

I was anything but content. I tried to be, but it just didn't stick. I thought marriage would level me off. I thought money would level me off. I thought being a good comic would make me fit into myself better, but nothing really did. My soul was always itchy.

When the irritation had become too much, I took a drastic action and enrolled in a philosophy class at the New School. The students in the class were a mix of women senior citizens going back to school and young people who didn't succeed in real college. The professor was a bald, beady-eyed, spectacled man with an aggressive, bitter demeanor and very little patience. Maybe he didn't succeed in real college either. He handed out a self-published pamphlet of his writings that was to be the text of the class.

I still had a romanticized Beatnik idea of what philosophy class would be. I thought we would all hang out and grapple with a collective existential discomfort while bonding together against a cold world. We would solve big problems and perhaps start a movement. A café society of a cranky dreamer, three grandmothers, two dim kids, and myself. I also thought that my propensity toward bad behavior in a classroom situation had dissipated with age, as had my inability to fully understand the tenets of philosophy. Within the first few meetings of the class, I was lost. I would show up stoned and made cracks at the professor's expense.

After the fourth class I was waiting for the elevator with the professor. I was wearing a hat that somehow implied I was a comedian; it was a jester's hat. Actually, it was a baseball cap that had the logo of the New York Comedy Festival printed above the bill. My teacher looked at the top of my head and asked, "Are you a comedian?"

"Yes," I said. "Do you like comedy?" Trying to kiss up.

"Comedy is fine," he said. "Are you taking my class for material or to learn philosophy?" He looked at me as if what defined me as a person was riding on my answer.

"I don't think there is a difference," I said. "My head feels pretty full when I leave." In retrospect, a very stoned thing to say.

"You can fill your head two ways," he said precisely, without missing a beat. "You can put new things into it or you can heat up what is already in there so it expands."

I chuckled uncomfortably, not sure whether I had been insulted or not. I had. I was an expander. That was the last day I went to class. I had learned enough.

It was also during this time that I came out as a Jew on stage. I had never really brought it up because I couldn't think of a way to do it that wouldn't reinforce the stereotype of what being a Jew was. I can't stand comedy that trivializes the Jewish type into a set of pathetic behavioral idiosyncrasies, i.e., Jews like to eat, Jews like to whine, Jews like to sit, Jews feel guilty, etc.

I was on stage in North Carolina. There were three hundred people in the room and no one was laughing at anything I was saying. I was bombing, badly. Sweat was spraying out of my head, which in retrospect might have been why I was bombing. It's weird when it sprays. Then, when I was right in the middle of delivering a joke, I stopped and said, "You know what? I'm a Jew," just to see what would happen, because I was down South and because I hate myself. Then, right after I said it, a guy in the front row sitting right beneath me turned to his wife and said, "I knew it." Like whatever led up to that statement was a healthy mental process. I couldn't help but push my luck. I was already in the soup. So I said, "You know what? I think the Christians are getting a bad dossier on the Jews. I think there's some misinformation going around, and I want to clear some stuff up because I'm here to help. Let's start with holidays. For instance, the Jews have Passover and you Christians have whatever it is you do with the Bunny. Oh, yeah, but we're the ones with the freaky rituals. Go find the colored eggs, kids, then you can eat a chocolate rabbit. Yeah, the Jews are the freaks. Sit on the fat guy's lap and ask him for free shit. Yeah, we're the weird ones." Then I said, "If you don't know what Passover is, it's a ritual dinner where we have a service and then there's a meal and then there's a sacrifice of a Christian baby, and then dessert." Some people laughed; others turned to the person sitting next to them and said, "I've heard that. You see what he's doing? He's telling the truth and he's twisting it to make it funny. He's manipulating the truth like a Jew."

I eventually appeared on an HBO half-hour special that Grandma Goldy said "was a little filthy," which killed me. She died before I could make it up to her. I became a regular on *Late Night with Conan O'Brien*. I appeared on the *Late Show with David Letterman*. Comedy Central even allowed me back. In other words, a career unfolded, slowly. I eased into my anger over time. There is a realization one makes as one gets older. When you're young you really think you are angry for reasons and causes. As you get older, you realize you might just be angry. It was part of my voice. I still craved a purpose. A grand purpose. I felt that God had put me on hold.

11

ONE morning the purpose arrived. I got a message from my old friend Jim. I hadn't heard from him since my wedding. "Marc, it's Jimmy. I'm in Israel, man. I got a job out here working for the ambassador. I'm engaged to an Israeli girl named Oriella. You and Kim ought to think about coming out. I got diplomatic plates on the car. We can go anywhere, man. Oriella speaks Hebrew. You guys can stay with us. We'll take two four-day weekends and see the whole country. It'll be beautiful. So, if you can, man, swing by."

What I heard underneath Jim's invitation was God reaching out again. God was using Jim and my Panasonic answering machine as conduits. That's when I was infected with full-blown Jerusalem Syndrome. I had had symptoms before, but had thought, *Israel, Jim, how clear does it have to be? There are no coincidences. I'm Grandma Goldy's number one. I'm the Kol Nidre kid. I had gone too far. This is the further instruction I was waiting for. Finally!*

I believed that if I were to go to Israel, there was a real good chance that God would assign me a task of a biblical level. He would pass on some information that I would bring back to the people and possibly change the course of the world. I'm serious.

I didn't know how it might happen. Maybe stone tablets in the Sinai; or perhaps God keeps up with the new technology and I would be delivered a divine disc. As long as it wasn't Mac, I could run it.

It didn't seem unreasonable to me. God used to talk to people all the time. Hell, he'd spoken to me before, just not recently. Read the Old Testament, the New Testament: Every other day it's "Abraham, this is God. I need you to do something for me. I need the kid. Thanks, I knew I could count on you. Bring him to the mountain, that's it, lay him out on the altar. Good. Raise the knife up. Good, good, now—wait, just kidding. Just testing you, Abe. Thanks for playing along. You're okay by me."

Who's God talking to now? I don't know. Once when I was walking through Times Square, I thought maybe God is talking to those guys you see roaming the streets talking to themselves. You know, those guys that are throwing their arms up in the air, screaming, "I can't! I can't, you bastard. No, I can't."

Maybe the other side of that conversation is God bearing down on them, saying, "You're the new leader."

"I can't. No. I can't!" they scream.

They're not crazy. They're reluctant prophets. Better give them a quarter.

God has chosen bad Jews before. Weren't they all a little bad? I mean, Noah must have done something wrong to get that job. Forty days and forty nights on that boat walking around saying, "It smells like shit on this boat! Not just shit! Every kind of animal shit. Times two! Look, I'm sorry I fucked her. Can we dock this thing? Soon? Please?"

I believed God had chosen me.

Of course, I didn't tell my wife this. There are some things you just don't tell your spouse. If I had said, "Honey, we are going to Israel and there's a real good chance that God is going to choose me for an assignment of some kind," I know what would've happened. There would've been a long conversation about medication, and I didn't need it. So, I just said, "Honey, we're going to Israel. Won't that be fun?" She was excited. She's a little Jewier than I am.

Everything was confirmed the night after I talked to

Jim. I had a vision. An honest-to-God, kicking-it old-school biblical-style vision. No magic powder involved. That was behind me.

I bolted up out of sleep, covered in sweat. My heart was pounding, and I was breathing fast. There was a strange white light filling the bedroom. There it was, floating over my bed in a swirling blue mist, about the size of a small car, turning slowly around: a giant camcorder. Floating next to it was a very old man with a long white beard wearing a pointed hat and a coat of stars that seemed to blend in with the sky. He was presenting the camera with his hands, as if it were a prize on a game show. He was rocking his head back and forth, sort of singing, "Good, love, good, love, good, love," in a droning repetition.

I knew at the time that it wasn't a commercial. They don't have that technology—*yet*. I didn't wake my wife up because, again, there are some things you don't tell wives. You don't wake your wife up in the middle of the night and say, "Do you see the giant camcorder, honey?" If I had done that, I would definitely be on medication.

The old man was laughing and singing when the vision disappeared, and I heard my wife saying, "What's the matter? Why are you up? Are you alright? Did you do drugs?"

"No, no," I said. "I'm fine. Go back to sleep."

But what did the vision mean? What was God trying to tell me?

I went back to sleep. When I woke up, I walked into the living room, where my wife was reading the Sunday paper. I leaned over her shoulder to give her a kiss, and when I looked down at the paper, right in front of me was an ad: Sony camcorder on sale, $850, at The Wiz. *It was the camcorder from the vision.* There are no coincidences. The *Wiz* was the guy in the dream—come on, it was a *sign*. My wife saw it as a sale, but that's really semantics. It was better that she didn't know.

It was finally clear to me. I was going to travel to Israel and God was going to show me his face and I would get it on tape. I was going to make the most important documentary ever. I needed that camcorder.

A couple of hours later, my wife and I walked into The Wiz. I don't know if this happens to anybody else, but when I walk into a place like that, I get that immediate sensation of "Hey, am I going to get fucked?"

I don't know if it's all the complicated electronic equipment or if it's the way the creepy sales staff is perched at the counter waiting to pounce. They don't hire people at these places, they *cast* them.

There's always the one older guy with a potbelly, slicked-back hair, tie, and a pocket protector. He's a heart attack waiting to happen. He looks like my Grandpa Jack. He's been selling air conditioners for twenty years. You are sure there is a picture of him in a photo album somewhere with a lei around his neck and a hula girl at his side from an appliance junket to Hawaii in the seventies. He's there to accommodate the old school.

"I'm Frank, the manager. How are ya? What can we help you find today?"

There are also always the younger, groovier guys to accommodate the younger, groovier people. Maybe they have a ponytail and a goatee. They also have assorted ethnic types to deal with the assorted ethnic types that come in. That number will be smaller or larger depending on the ethnic profile of the neighborhood.

Kim and I were looking at the cameras, and of course Groovy Guy ambled up. "Hey, you two. Checking out the camcorders? Right on. If you have any questions, I'll be right here behind you. My name is Scott."

"Scott, is this the one on sale for eight hundred and fifty dollars?" I said like a person who knows what he needs.

They always say the same thing. "No, that one you're

looking at is a hundred thousand dollars. We're out of the one on sale." I was devastated. "What? We just saw it in the—" Kim cut me off.

"Marc, come here a second." She pulled me aside. "That's a bait and switch. He can't do that. It's illegal."

"What are you talking about?" I whined.

"I saw it on *Sixty Minutes*. It's a bait and switch. I'm going to say something. It's wrong."

She was going in. I could see it in her eyes. She was going to make things right. She did that sometimes, and whenever she did I would usually go elsewhere in the store until the problem had passed.

Kim walked back over to Groovy Guy and locked eyes with him. "We saw a Sony camcorder in the paper advertised for eight hundred and fifty dollars, and now that we're here, you say you don't have it and are trying to sell us a more expensive camera. That's a bait and switch, and that's illegal."

"No, ma'am, we're just out of the other camera." He still thought he had a chance.

Kim stepped closer and upped the intensity of her gaze. She's like a cobra. She'll lock you in and hold you there until you do the right thing. I'd been locked in it for almost ten years.

"I don't think you understand," Kim emphasized. "I will take you down if you don't find me one of those camcorders we saw advertised."

I was watching the scene unfold from behind the camera-bag rack. Groovy Guy stood his ground for about seven seconds, then buckled. "Uh, I think I might have one more in the back," he said, and disappeared into the stockroom.

I ran out from behind the bags and hugged Kim. "Good job, baby. I knew he had one back there." I didn't know any such thing. I was ready to buy the expensive one.

"Yeah, we got him," she said, satisfied with herself.

He brought out the box, set it on the counter, and said, "Here's the Sony."

"Sony," I blurted. "It's good. It's love." I shot a smile over to Kim.

I looked at the box as if it solved all my problems forever. I thought there should've been a chorus of angels, but there wasn't. Just Groovy Guy, and he said, "I need to ask if you want the in-store warranty. If something goes wrong with the camera within the first year, anything, we'll fix it or replace it for free—for a hundred dollars more."

I thought about it for a second. "The math doesn't really work out on that, does it? Doesn't it have its own warranty?" I said. "It's a Sony. It's good. It's love."

"Why do you keep saying that?" Kim whispered, embarrassed.

"I don't know," I said to her. "Look, we don't want the in-store warranty," I said in a finalizing tone to Groovy Guy.

"You don't want the warranty?" he said, suddenly exasperated for some reason. "Really? Okay, I have to get my manager."

"Okay, whatever you have to do," I said.

"Frank!" he screamed.

Then air conditioner guy came over.

"Yeah, what? What's the problem, Scott?"

"They don't want the warranty."

Frank looked overly surprised. Then it started to unfold like a poorly rehearsed play. He actually said, "No warranty? Hmm, I've never heard of that before. No warranty?"

"Nope," Groovy Guy said smugly. "They said they didn't want it."

"Now, I can't understand why you wouldn't want the warranty," Frank said earnestly. "Hang on a sec. José! Leroy! Achmed! Come over here. This guy doesn't want the warranty. Maybe you guys could help me understand this."

Then this multi-culti cabal of appliance salesmen assembled before me in what looked like a dance line. It felt like the end of a musical.

Leroy says, "No warranty?" in a hip-hop tone.

Achmed says, "No warranty?" with an Arabic accent.

José just says, "No guarantía?"

They all join together singing, "No warranty! He doesn't want the warranty!"

My voice rises above them in a crescendo and stops them. "No, I don't want the warranty. It's SONY. It's GOOD. It's LOVE. It's bigger than all of us, and it's MINE. It's OURS. Good-bye, we're off."

Finale. Curtain. My wife and I walk out.

Next stop was Niketown. Kim wanted to get some shoes. I didn't want to go there. I don't really like Nikes. Their politics bother me. Sweatshops? Who wants that karma on their feet? She went to the women's department, and I went browsing up in the hiking area. I was passively looking around when I saw it, the vision of shoe illumination. The perfect sneaker/hiking boot hybrid. It was sitting on a shelf, alone, glowing, resonating, like the burning bush. I knew then that it was what God wanted me to wear in Israel. I ran up to the shelf and pulled it down. I thought, *I don't care if they're held together with Third World spit. I am meant to have this shoe.* I ran up to the salesclerk, held the shoe in front of me and asked, "Do you have these in a size twelve?"

He said, "Calm down. I'll check. Please get out of the stockroom."

He came out with the box and pulled the perfect shoes out of it and put them on my feet. I started to walk around. I said, "These are amazing. I feel great, whole."

"They feel alright?" he said.

"Alright? They feel amazing. I'm never taking them off." I started stomping around the store.

"Sir, could you please take it easy? You're making the other customers nervous."

"These are the most powerful shoes I've ever had on. They should come with a cape," I said proudly. "I'll take them."

"You want to wear them out, sir?"

"Wear them out? I'm gonna wear them to sleep," I said. "You can throw those other shoes away."

I walked around and found Kim. I showed her my shoes, beaming as if I were ten years old. She hadn't found anything for herself. I took the camera out of the box in the foyer of Niketown. After we left the store, I swear people were parting as we walked down Fifty-seventh Street. In retrospect, it might've been because I was skip-stomping down the sidewalk like a hyperactive child, in my pretty new boots as I watched people passing by on the little screen that winged out of the side of my camcorder.

These are the trials and tribulations.

12

WE flew to Israel on El Al airlines. If you go to Israel, you've got to fly El Al. It's in the Talmud.

El Al is a very high-security operation. There are three or four security checkpoints. There are armed Mossad agents with Uzis. When you go through that much security, you actually have a moment when you say, "We don't have a bomb, do we, honey? You packed. Is there anything that looks like a bomb? Honey, tell me, we're almost at the guy with the gun."

I stepped up to the counter. "We don't have a bomb." He motions me to the side. "Why do I have to step aside? She packed."

This security ritual prepares you for entering a culture in which an abandoned gym bag is a national security threat. It's *that* tense.

I generally have some fear of flying, but when you fly to Israel there are always at least two Hasidim davening in the back of the plane. I figured they've got the direct line to the Almighty. We were covered. Aside from that, God had to know *I* was on the plane.

We actually were seated next to a rabbi, and I told him about my vision. I told him God had chosen me and I showed him my shoes and my camera. He took the camera in his hands and looked it over for about five minutes. Then he looked at me earnestly and told me he had a brother-in-law who could have given me a better deal.

We spent ten hours on the plane. During those ten hours I read the camcorder manual cover to cover and made notes in the margins. I learned how to work every element of my camcorder *and* I skimmed the kabala. I wanted to cover all my bases.

Now, I hadn't seen Jim in *three years.* I'd *never* met his girlfriend. When we arrived in Tel Aviv, I walked off the plane with the camera stuck to my eye socket. I saw Jim. "Hey, Jimmy, we're here. Israel! No, stay there. Wave. I got a good shot here. Yeah, it's a new camcorder. Is that Oriella? Hi, Marc, nice to meet you. Stay there. We'll hug in a minute. Great shot. Okay, you guys just walk ahead. I want to get this. Where we going now? Baggage! That'll be great." We get to the luggage carousel.

My wife said, "Is that ours?"

"Hold on. I'll check."

I clicked the zoom button on the top of the camera. It slowly moved in on the bag. "Yep, that's it. This is a great zoom. I can read the name tag."

I followed the bag around the carousel with the camera. "Aren't you going to get it, honey?"

Kim shot me the look, like a cobra.

"What? Why are you looking at me like that?" I put down the camera and picked up the bag.

We went to their apartment. It was a nice place. We spent two days in Tel Aviv and I decided God would definitely not hang out in Tel Aviv. It's a big city. It's not very interesting or ancient. It is right down the road from Jaffa, the oldest port in the world. It was where Jonah popped out of the fish onto the beach. Kim and I walked up there. I looked down at the beach, trying to imagine a busy port going about port business when, out of nowhere, this giant fish surfaces and spits out this guy who wipes the slime off himself and segues into a lecture about how everyone is doomed. What a great opening. What a day that must've been. People talking for years about the guy who was spit out of the fish to set up his bit about trouble and repentance. When Kim and I were in Jaffa, there wasn't much to see. Just some ruins and an uninspired museum.

I was itching to get on the road.

Going on the road as an adult was a much different experience for me than it was when I was younger. Your Bohemian crew turns into "My wife and I and another couple." It's very humbling and much more predictable, as is much of adulthood.

The first day out we drove through the desert of the Holy Land. It's *all* desert. It was beautiful. The first stop is the Jordan River, where Christ and many people bathed early on; the mighty River Jordan mentioned in many an old spiritual melody. I should make it clear at this point that I'm no biblical scholar. I have random facts about random places, some not even true. I choose to get my information secondhand, as opposed to from a reliable source. It's more interesting that way and I've never liked doing homework.

We decided to bathe in the River Jordan ourselves. I was up to my waist, walking against the current. The camera was wedged into my face. I was thinking that camcorders should really come with an accessory that clamps the camera to your head, like a cybernetic digital claw that interfaces your consciousness with the machinery of the camera and sends the footage directly from your brain to your home computer via the Internet. Then you could use your hands, eat, and you would never need to stop taping. You know they're working on it up at the campus.

I was in the water, zooming in on the reeds. I was panning along the river's edge, I was shooting upstream, I was looking for babies in baskets, I was looking for some indication that I was on the trail of God. I got *nothing*. I did get a God tone, though, but that was easy to get in Israel.

We were all standing in the river talking when the strangest thing happened. A Hasid came floating down the river wearing his pants, shoes, tallit, pancho, and yarmulke, laughing. He got about thirty feet upstream from us, saw us, pulled himself to the side of the river, and climbed out, then disappeared into the bushes. This happened with about twenty Hasidim. I thought for a moment *Maybe that's where Hasidim come from, a spring in the Jordan River.* We were baffled until we saw a few of them in the bushes gawking at Kim and Oriella, who were wearing bikinis, and we realized they're not allowed to look upon women so scantily clad. It was a bit bizarre to see their excited faces with their payes dangling, peering through the reeds until we'd spot them and they'd scurry off and reappear about thirty feet downstream from us, emerge from the bushes, and get back into the water and continue floating.

I just couldn't believe they were wearing their yarmulkes in the river. Why do they wear them all the time? *We get it.* They're Jews. Maybe it's so God doesn't lose them in a crowd. "Where are the good Jews? Oh, there they are, with the hats. In the bushes, oh, those are a few bad good Jews. I'll make note of it. I'm so glad I thought of the hats. I'm a genius. I am God."

We all got out of the river and dried off. We were walking along the path beside the river to go back to the car when I heard a bunch of male voices yelling playfully from the water. I knew it was them. I turned on the camera and did a voice-over. "We are stalking the Hasidim in the wild. This is where you may find them, along the banks of the River Jordan." We turned a corner on the path and there they were, about forty of them hanging from the trees, splashing in the water. It was a great shot.

"Where are we going now?" I asked as we all climbed into the car.

"Megiddo," Jim said.

Onward then into Megiddo, the valley of Armageddon, where the big bad multiheaded beast of Revelation is to bring in the biblical period of darkness.

(I like the Christian landmarks because that's where things are still going to happen.) I stood and looked over the valley, waiting for something, seeing if my presence there was what was needed to get things rocking.

I was holding the camera in anticipation. I panned across the valley slowly, once, twice, three times. *Nothing.* I jumped up and down. *Nothing.* Kim said, "What are you doing?" I told her I was stretching. Then, some Greek tourists asked us to take their picture. "Who sent you here?" I asked suspiciously. They did not understand. I decided they were not a sign. They didn't seem very menacing and they had the right number of heads between them. I took their picture and we moved on.

Oddly, right outside of the valley of Armageddon there's a McDonald's, the Megiddo McDonald's. Which led me to believe that perhaps the apocalypse already happened. It just wasn't as big as we thought it was going to be. Maybe it wasn't *billions killed*—just eaten.

I generally don't eat McDonald's, because I don't believe in it, but we hadn't eaten in a while. So we went in. I had a Big Machh and fries and, of course, a Cokechh. Fueled, we went onward into the Golan Heights.

The Golan Heights is the border territory between Israel and Syria that has shifted back and forth over the years and continues to be a hot zone to this day. Many people have died there. There are hundreds of acres of unusable land because of live and unexcavated mines. That is where the reality of Israel started to seep from my camcorder to my head. The military necessities of Zionism have always made me nervous. It's one of the reasons I had avoided going to Israel. It's scary.

I understand Zionism, vaguely. My parents were sofa Zionists; the kind that sit on the couch watching the news and say, "Something's wrong in Israel. Get the checkbook."

I remember being in third grade in Hebrew school. The teacher came in and announced, "Okay, next week everyone needs to bring in five dollars. We're sending the money to Israel to plant a tree for your grandparents. Don't forget to wear your Purim costumes. Shalom, remember that means "hello" and "good-bye." Shalom, Aaron. Shalom, Joshua. Shalom, Cheryl. Shalom, Joshua Two. Shalom, Marc with a 'c.' "

I thought when I got off the plane in Israel, *I want to see my grandpa's tree.* But as an adult I realized there was probably no tree. There might be a Grandpa Jack artillery shell or a Grandma Goldy rocket launcher. Or perhaps they put all the money together to build Yahrzeit missiles that have commemorative plaques on the side of them that light up if they're shot off on the day of that Yahrzeit.

Coming down through the Golan Heights, we came upon a bombed-out mosque. It was an Islamic shrine that had been hit by an artillery shell, probably during the Six-Day War. Half of the mosque was caved in. I got a camera angle on it. I was glib at first: "Muhammad has left the building."

Then we went under the barbed-wire fence and entered the mosque itself. To see that type of destruction up close is devastating. It's like the first time you go to an auto junkyard. To think that there might have been people in there when it hit. I stood in this mosque. I turned the camera off. I thought, *Am I a part of this? Am I? Is this where my five dollars went?*

A fear set in. I was not only looking to the sky for the face of God but for missiles as well.

13

THE next day we went to Masada. Thank God for ancient ruins. They can be a relief. Masada was the refuge for the Jews during the first revolt. Nine hundred plus Jews holed up in King Herod's summer home and held their own against 15,000 Roman soldiers, and when they were about to be overrun, instead of captivity or death at the hands of the Romans, they chose mass suicide. Today the ruins stand as a monument to Jewish heroism. It's also a very nice day hike.

We were hiking up the path to the top of Masada, where there is a breathtaking view of the Dead Sea. By this time, I was walking far ahead of my wife and friends. I was barely speaking to them. I spoke solely to my camcorder. My camcorder and I had bonded and were having a great time. I hiked up the path in my perfect shoes, taping everything and talking nonstop. "Look, I could fall here. That would be bad." I zoomed to the ground. "Hey, a spider. A big Israeli spider."

I had surrendered my will to a small 1½-by-2-inch viewfinder. That was the context of my experience. I was walking through an illusion that I controlled and could hold in my hand. *I* was the Jewish king of this very small land.

I got to the top before the others. I lit a cigarette. It was about 150 degrees outside. My skin was melting. I had the Dead Sea framed in my small square universe as I panned the region. "It's beautiful, isn't it?" I asked the camera.

Then, a miracle happened. *The camera just broke!* It made a clicking sound, followed by a breaking apart of the image on the screen, followed by a whirring noise, and then it just fizzled out. I screamed, "You gotta be kidding. This isn't happening. We're only four days out."

My wife walked up. "What's the matter, baby?" she asked innocently.

"The fucking camera broke," I squalled. "There's no point now. We gotta go home." I was pacing and looking at the camera.

"What are you talking about?" She was immediately irritated.

"I was gonna look God in the face," I yelled. "And get it on tape."

"Maybe we should get you into the shade," she said, concerned.

Then I had that moment when I just wanted to throw the camera over the edge. You know, when something mechanical breaks and you just want to break it more to show it who's boss? Then I thought ahead and pictured the humiliation of looking over the edge and saying, "It's really broken now, honey. I can see it down there. Maybe I should go down and get it."

I didn't do that. I dropped down to my knees and prayed to Sony.

"Please work, Sony. I know you're a good product. Please, Sony, bring the camcorder back to me."

I shook the camcorder. I pushed all of the buttons. I coddled it. I even kissed it. I tried to blow the digital breath of life into the camera, but I don't have it in me. I hunched over the camera in my hands, defeated.

Then I realized, *Hey, wait a minute*. This might be exactly what I was waiting for. Maybe this was God saying, "Put the camera down. Don't have a mediated experience. Look at Israel through your own eyes and your heart. Get down on your hands and knees and kiss the ground of the homeland as a Jew."

That's what I thought God was saying. So, I said, "Okay, I get it. I hear you. Hang on a minute. Sony is fucking me! Not just *Sony* but *The Wiz* is fucking me! The Wiz is an evil wizard! I knew I was going to get fucked! No warranty, of course. My camera came off of the no-warranty-shit shelf!"

So, then I astral-projected myself back to The Wiz. I didn't know if I still could, but it's like riding a bike. You never forget how. I flew over deserts, mountains, oceans, and continents in a matter of seconds. I flew right through the doors of The Wiz and grabbed Groovy Guy by the ponytail and began bashing his head against the counter. I dragged him around the store by the hair. I screamed, "Is there a camera in here that works so I can tape you crying, you fucking asshole?!"

Then I flew out of the store, up Madison to Fifty-fifth Street to the Sony headquarters. Right past security. "I got a problem with a product. Put the guns down!" On into the corner office and into the face of the executive in charge of ruining my vacation who stood between me and the Almighty. "I believed in your product. I had faith in the quality of your product. I had hope for spiritual enlightenment through your product, and it fucking broke. Now you have to reckon with me!"

Then, everything started spinning. Apparently I had

been out of my body too long. I heard my old friend Nancy's voice from the Green House echoing in my head: "That's called astral projection. Don't fuck with that. Don't fuck with that. Don't fuck with that." Then, like Dorothy, I was back on the top of Masada, holding my camcorder like Hamlet held the skull. "Where be your jibes now? Your gambols? Your songs? Your flashes of merriment, that were wont to set the table on a roar?"

I was so sad. My wife and friends tried to comfort me, but I was inconsolable. They had no idea of the scope of the problem. How it could affect the future of the world.

The next day we stopped at the Sea of Galilee. It's more like a lake. They have waterskiing and bars and restaurants on the beach. We waded out into the water and went swimming. While no one was looking I made a sad attempt to walk on water. It didn't work. The people who were sitting at the bar on the patio behind me laughed. It's a very awkward thing to be caught trying something like that.

I felt vulnerable and scared without my camcorder. I felt out of control, ungrounded as we headed up into the north again to visit my wife's friend Elana, who lives on a settlement.

As best I can tell, settlers, whether they are secular or nonsecular, are basically pioneering nationalists who go up into the middle of nowhere, build a few houses, call it a town, and enable the Israeli government to say, "We can't have Arabs up there. There are already Jews in place."

We get to the town of four houses. It's up on a ridge. It's isolated and desolate. We get to their house, where the mood is somber and full of a commitment I don't get. I wanted my camcorder to work. It protected me from engaging with my immediate experience. It gave me purpose. I couldn't handle the unmediated reality of Israel. I realized I'd much rather watch it at home on my VCR in my apartment in Queens. There, where Christians, Jews, and Muslims live under one roof with very little difficulty, unless there's a boiler problem, when we rise up against the Dominican landlord, but that's a completely different political struggle.

I was really beginning to unravel.

"Why do you live up here? Is it safe? What do you guys do for fun? How do you get food up here? Do they fly it in? I didn't see any restaurants. Where do you rent videos? Where's the mall? I don't understand why you live like this. Where are we going to sleep?" I ranted on in mild panic.

"We have no room here because of the kids," Elana

said, "but we've reserved you guys a room at a hostel in Sachnin, the Arab city down the road."

"Arab city?" I said. "Arabs? Aren't they the bad guys?" I'm not racist. I was just nervous and ill informed.

"They're Israeli Arabs, not Palestinians," Jim said. "It'll be fine."

"Fine. Right."

On the way to Sachnin I kept picturing how easy it is to die in Israel. We could be driving down an isolated road and some masked men could stop the car and drag us out. "Bism Allah! Bism Allah!" There would be guns pressed to the backs of our heads and we'd all be executed and left to rot as a political statement.

I didn't want to go out that way. I don't want that kind of press. "Funnyman Marc Maron dies in mysterious Israeli border dispute outside Palestinian territories. Everything was just finally starting to turn around for Marc when he was caught in an ambush dot-dot-dot." I'm not that committed.

When we got to Sachnin, the road seemed to weave around for miles. There were no stores, no lights, no gas stations; no familiar brand logos lit up to show signs of life and hope. We pulled into a dirt driveway alongside a large three-story stucco house. The top floor of the house

looked unfinished because there was no glass in the win-
dows. A man came out to greet us. The "hostel" was the
redone basement of his house.

Everything seemed to be cushioned. The walls, floors,
and ceiling all seemed to have a pillow-like feel to them.
I couldn't sleep. My heart was racing, my mind was pacing. It was like a hundred and ninety degrees and there
were bugs crawling on my face. I felt like slamming my
head against the wall, which would've been okay, since it
was cushioned.

In the morning we all went up to the top floor of the
house, which, as it turned out, was intentionally unfinished. It was like a giant patio. The owner's wife and
daughter served us a breakfast of pita bread, a slice of sad-
looking bologna, scrambled eggs that were overcooked
and drenched in oil, and sweet stewed olives.

The eight-year-old daughter of the man who owned
the hostel walked us around the town. The streets were
teeming with activity of day-to-day business. It felt fes-
tive, unlike the settlement. Everyone was out doing
things. There were animals being butchered in the street.
It was very homey. People were coming up to us, inviting
us into their homes, giving us coffee, and trying to communicate with us. They were so nice. They don't see
many Americans.

We left Sachnin the following morning and headed back to Tel Aviv. In the car I had a new mantra: "Gotta get the camcorder fixed, gotta get the camcorder fixed, gotta get the camcorder fixed." That was all I could think about. The camcorder had to be functional when we went to Jerusalem. I thought that whatever was to happen between God and me would certainly happen in Jerusalem.

When we got back to Jim's apartment, I looked in the Tel Aviv yellow pages under "Sony." I found a Sony repair center. I went alone to the Sony repair center. I walked in. I don't know what was going on that day, or if every day was like that, but there were literally hundreds of people mobbed in front of the counter. It almost seemed like some sort of revolt against Sony. People were waving boom boxes, Walkmans, televisions, and camcorders above their heads. There was shouting. There was chaos. It almost seemed that all Sony products broke on the same day for everyone, and don't think I didn't think that.

Behind the counter there were these four panicked, sweating Israeli geeks trying to accommodate the uprising. Behind the geeks, going back farther than the eye could see, were shelves upon shelves of unrepaired Sony products. It looked like a grand cathedral of broken electronic equipment. I tried to make my way through the crowd but couldn't, so I mosh-pitted myself atop the crowd and was carried to the counter, where I delivered the camcorder into the sweaty hands of one of the geeks. He looked at the camcorder, he looked at the shelves behind him, and then he looked at me and shook his head and said, "Oh, no, eight weeks."

"No," I said. "Today."

"No, no, I cannot," he said.

"I'm an American," I said. "I'm here on vacation."

Somehow that translated to "Please don't help me, ever," as I was swallowed up by the crowd and spat back out onto the street, holding my crippled camcorder.

We had to leave for Jerusalem the following day. I thought about buying another camcorder, but it would've cost a fortune and the machines there operate by different format. They take pictures right to left. It would've been useless in the States.

I was really beginning to give up the struggle. I was trying to let go of the idea of the camera working again. I was trying to just adjust to being without it. I was trying to engage with and enjoy my wife and friends. It wasn't sticking.

When we got to Jerusalem I immediately looked up electronic repair in the yellow pages. I found Avram's. I gave the phone book to Oriella to translate. "Does it say 'Sony'?"

She said, "Yes, Marc, it says 'Sony.' "

"Yes!" I yelped.

We all went immediately to Avram's. It was a small electronic repair shop. I walked in. My first thought was, *Am I going to get fucked? On a smaller scale?*

Avram was a big, happy, gregarious Israeli. I showed him the camcorder. I was in a panic. "I don't know what happened. I was just holding it. It's very important to everyone that this works here."

"This is no problem," he said. "I fix today. Come back, two hours."

"Thank you. You really don't realize how important this is."

While we were waiting, we went to a market to get some fruit. It amazed me how people in Israel have their blinders up to just how scary it is to be there. As we stood there looking at fruit, my friend Jim told me that some people were killed in that market by a bomb a few weeks before. I said, "Well, put the fucking plum down. Let's get out of here. I'm just not that committed. I can live without the fruit."

Two hours later, I was back at Avram's. I ran in. He smiled big.

"It is fixed, my friend."

"Thanks. You might have saved the world."

I paid him. He looked at me and said, "My friend, relax. Don't worry. You're in Israel."

I don't know in what world those three phrases fit together, but I tried to relax. I couldn't. I was elated that my camcorder was working. My head was tingling.

It *was* working, but it didn't have that organic Sony feel to it anymore. It felt as if he may have wedged a toothpick or a piece of gum into some mechanism. It *was* working, though, and we *were* in Jerusalem.

Jerusalem was where I thought it was going to happen. Whatever I was waiting for would happen there. Jerusalem is the mystical navel of the universe. All of the corporate headquarters of the Western world's religions are there. If they're not there, they at least have a franchise there. Obviously the Vatican isn't located there, but the Church of the Holy Sepulchre serves as an embassy. [That's where they took Jesus off the cross after he was walked around in that awkward way.] The Wailing Wall is there for the Jews. It's actually called the "Western Wall" now, because we're not upset anymore. The reason the Jews pray at the Wall is because it's as close as they can get to the Temple Mount, the site of Solomon's Temple

and the Second Temple, the holiest place in the Jewish religion. Once the temple is rebuilt, they can pray there
once again. There will be no construction in the foresee-
able future because the Dome of the Rock, the third-holi-
est shrine of Islam, sits on the Temple Mount. The
Messiahs for the Jews and the Christians can't come back
until that temple is rebuilt, and apparently, the Dome of
the Rock is causing landing problems. These are ancient
and seemingly unresolvable mystical problems that I have
no solution for. I saw Jerusalem as a religious theme park
where I wanted to go on all the rides. And I did.

The Church of the Holy Sepulchre is chaos. When we
walked in, there were hundreds of people mobbed
around the many religious relics throughout the interior
of the church. There were people and dangling Christian
symbols everywhere. The last five Stations of the Cross
are all within the church: where the Christ was stripped,
where they nailed him up, where they lifted the cross,
where they took him down, and where they laid him in a
tomb. We took the tour and the last stop was the marble
slab where Christ's body was laid and anointed before it
was placed in the tomb. People were surrounding the
slab, some placing their jewelry and religious trinkets on
the marble top and moving those items around. I guess

the idea was to charge their stuff up with the power of the dead Christ. I placed my camcorder on the marble and moved it around a bit. I figured it couldn't hurt.

The Temple Mount is by far the most awesome place I visited in Israel. Time seemed to stand still when we were within the confines of the Temple Mount area. It is an expansive flat space that was clearly designated to accommodate a huge structure. In the center of the space stands the Dome of the Rock mosque. It is a beautiful building covered in mosaic and gold leaf. I walked around the area surrounding the dome. I was taping. I felt the Gray come over me. I was standing on the holiest ground on Earth. God knew I was there. *Soon, I will be contacted*, I thought. Kim and I asked Jim to take our picture. I put my arm around her, and out of nowhere a Moslem man came over, removed my arm from my wife, and shook his head. No public displays of affection are allowed on the Temple Mount unless they are for Allah.

The last ride I went on was the Western Wall.

I stood at the wall with the davening Hasidim. I felt awkward standing there. I didn't know what to do. I looked at the Hasidim. I've always thought they were arrogant. They think they're the only real Jews. They do. It trickles down from there. The Orthodox don't believe that the Conservative Jews are real Jews, and the

Conservatives don't believe that the Reform Jews are real Jews, but the people that hate and want to kill Jews think that we're all the same, so why do we help them by dividing and conquering ourselves? There are no mild hate groups that only target the Reform, and if there were, they would be looked down upon in the hate-group community as not being a *real* hate group. "Why can't you just hate everyone?" "We're just not that religious."

That's when I realized why the Hasidim were there. They are the extreme margin of Judaism. They justify the middle. There is no middle without them. They are there to keep the arcane channels to God open through prayer and ritual round the clock. On some level, they are there for all Jews, everywhere, whether they like it or not. What if one Hasid at the Wall were to one day say, mid-daven, "You know what?" They all stop davening to hear. "Fuck it. Let's get out of here. Lose the hats, lose the beards, cut the curls. We're gone." And they all walk off forever.

Once word got out, how long would it be before all Jews around the world said, "*They* stopped? Well, can we all stop? It would save me a thousand a year on seats."

They need to be there. That is why Jerusalem is a living, mystical city. The Zionist State of Israel would be meaningless if it didn't have the heart of Judaism to protect. [The heart of Judaism would be vulnerable if the

Zionist State of Israel didn't exist.] If it did crumble, Jerusalem might become the ruins of a faded mystical city.

I have no political solutions. I think the wrong negotiator might have been chosen for the peace talks. Instead of Clinton, maybe they should have used Michael Ovitz and brought in Michael Eisner and put Jerusalem under the nondenominational control of a secular corporate neo-deity like Disney. Jerusalem would then become one of the "Happiest Places on Earth."

People could enjoy Jewishland, with its mechanical Hasidim. Then they could go to Christianland and ride the cross; then Moslemland: "Gotta take your shoes off for Moslemland. Mom, you can't come in." Biblical characters could wander around in period costume. "Get your slings ready, kids, here comes Goliath." And, of course, there would be Space Mountain. All Happiest Places on Earth have a Space Mountain, even if it doesn't fit in with the theme. There's always room for space and all the hope that it holds.

As I stood at the Wall I realized that I was part of an ancient, mystical, and spiritual community. I have my *own* beliefs, but at the wall I felt that I was part of an eternal legacy. It was something other than the Internet, which might ultimately win out, as it slowly usurps the collective unconscious.

I stopped taping because I wanted to put a note in the Wall. That's what people do if they're not Hasidim. You write a note to God and place it in a crack of the Wall. I wrote a very general note. HELP! I waited for a reply. Nothing.

I swear the guy next to me put his business card in the Wall. So tacky. I thought, *Do you have to live up to the stereotype here?*

I was so overwhelmed by the Wall that I had to immediately go out and buy a tallit. The tallit is the prayer shawl that most American Jews wear twice a year, if they can find it. On some level, Jerusalem is just a very large synagogue gift shop. If you don't have some kind of religious catharsis, you will be overwhelmed with the pressing desire to buy menorahs, mezuzahs, yarmulkes, and whatever tchotchkes are necessary to make you feel superior to your Jewish friends and family. "Oh, really? You've never been?"

When we left Jerusalem, I resumed taping. I knew I was close. *I could feel God.*

We drove through the Negev and crossed over into Jordan to visit Petra. When we crossed the border we were in the real desert. There were miles and miles of nothing but the occasional amazing rock formation and camel.

Petra is situated in the middle of the Jordanian desert. It encompasses the ruins of a very advanced ancient civilization. It was built thousands of years ago by the Nabataeans. Did you see the last Indiana Jones movie with Sean Connery? The Red City? That's Petra. It is spread across miles of beautiful red rock cliffs that are riddled with cliff dwellings. Not your run-of-the-mill Pueblo Indian caves in the rock cliff dwellings. These were ornate, detailed, architectural wonders chiseled delicately into the face of pure hot rock. There are actual Greek-style columns chiseled into the rock. Which isn't even necessary. Why? Someone must have come down from the north and said, "You know, they're doing something new in Greece." So the King probably said, "We must have these new columns."

The commitment that went into chiseling these things was intense. I mean, what could they have been using for tools? Spoons? It was either commitment or slavery. You don't want to think about that when you are standing in front of something beautiful. It undermines your aesthetic experience, as a tourist, to think there might have been some guy with a whip, saying, "Build the pretty thing!" Unless you're that kind of tourist.

Petra was a great hub of mysticism and commerce. There are the ruins of an outdoor theater, a technologically advanced water distribution system, and temples of a lost religion. Petra was at the cutting edge of desert culture in its day. I'm sure people would stand on their terraces in Petra's heyday and say, "We've got it all. I couldn't imagine living anywhere but here. Let's go to Zabar's."

And now there's nothing but ruins, artifacts.

We walked through this mile-long ravine along the overhanging cliffs on a path called the Siq. It was the main road into Petra. I was taping everything. All along the cliff walls were small eroded square reliefs that had faded symbols on them. The tour guide said they were called "god rocks" and they most likely were depictions of the gods of the culture. They don't know for sure, because to this day they don't know what religion was practiced by the Nabataeans. Petra *is* the ruins of a faded, mystical city. I raised my hand and suggested, "Maybe these are actually ancient billboards advertising a popular soft drink of the time. Is that possible?"

The guide looked at me the way an angry snake would and said, "No, it is *not.*"

We arrived at the highest point in Petra, which is called the "altar point," because it is an actual altar. The entire top of this hill was leveled off. In the center of the plane was a slab of red rock about the size of an adult male. It was surrounded by strange, geometrically aligned, pyramidal stair-like structures. It was believed that human sacrifices were made to appease the gods on that slab. I thought, *Man, that's deep.* I walked slowly around the altar, filming. I was fascinated. The thought that people could be that brutal and possessed by faith and fear was hard to handle. A sacrifice is performed by a priest or holy man, the seer, the illuminated one who understands more deeply than the rest. He understands that the ritual act done with the knowledge or in the presence of the followers will guarantee the power of the illusion he purports to understand and, conversely, guarantee his power over the followers.

A human sacrifice is the sacrifice of a life: a history of moments, movements, events, engagements, feelings, pains, pleasures, achievements, loves, visions, and hopes. Brought to an end on a slab of rock for the sake of something larger, a greater, godly agenda, a lie. The very possibility of such a thing was mind-blowing to me. As you know, I have a thing for altars. I stepped slowly around it. "They used to sacrifice human beings here. That's so intense."

I stepped onto the altar, pointed the camcorder skyward. Under my breath I said, "This would be a good time." I waited. Nothing.

Then, I stepped up onto a stone staircase above the altar. I put my camcorder in its bag and reached over to grab my wife's still camera to take a picture of the mountain in front of me. As I turned to take the picture, I heard the sound of my camcorder bouncing down the steps of the stone staircase. I heard all the delicate machinery and components clanking down those steps. I turned around to see my camcorder bounce right out onto the sacrificial altar and stop. When it hit the altar, I heard a voice behind me say, "There goes a thousand dollars." I turned to see who had said it. No one was there.

It was the voice of God.

I looked up and said, "Subtle."

It was over. The camera lay alone on the slab of rock. Other tourists began to gather around. I looked over at my wife and friends. They were glaring at me smugly, as if justice had at last been delivered.

I went to pick up the camcorder. It was really broken. The start button was all bashed in. I couldn't even shove it up Sony's ass anymore. What would I say? "I was holding it and it just started crinkling in on itself. I don't know. You take it. It's creepy."

I was standing on the altar, cradling the camera as if it were a child. I looked up into the sky that once harnessed the gods and demons that have defined spiritual belief for millions of people for thousands of years, and it was empty and red and beautiful. My camcorder was dead.

There was no face of God in sight. I realized deep within that I knew *nothing*. I stood on the altar and I felt naked, stupid, and a little used. I was a cosmic doofus, a sucker, a mark. Sony and God had been waiting for this to happen. I had been set up, caught in the middle; I was the catalyst and the punch line of a biblical struggle between good and evil. I blew the dust off of my camcorder, put it in the bag, and slouched slowly down from the altar point. It was done. I didn't get the job. I was free.

I had one more day to indulge in my vacation. We drove back down through Jordan and Elat, down into the Sinai to a small town on the coast of the Red Sea called Terebin. Oriella had visited there when she was a child, and it was still part of Israel. It wasn't so much a town as it was a dirt-cheap, run-down, low-rent tourist outpost. There was snorkeling and pedal boats, strewn garbage, dusty sand, broken-down trucks, stray dogs, and camels. There were three or four small, one-story hostels in a row. In front of each hostel was an open seating area with pillows, couches, low tables, and thatched roofs right at the edge of the water. Bedouin men served you as you sat. Mint tea, hummus, and tabouli.

We checked ourselves into a hostel. I was shattered and had surrendered. I felt the way the town looked.

My spiritual journey was over. I hated my camcorder, and I wasn't too happy with God or myself. Once we got settled in, we went out to sit. I tried to get reacquainted with my wife and friends.

While Jim, Kim, and Oriella were talking, I stepped away and pulled one of the Bedouin guys aside. I looked into his eyes and pinched my thumb and forefinger together and brought them to my lips and made the toke sound, the sucking in a joint noise, the universal sign language for "Can you get us some pot?"

He looked at me and said, "Yes, I get for you."

I said, "That would be great." I thought if I could score some reefer, it might make up for what an asshole I'd been the entire trip, and besides, I needed the relief.

It must have been about two in the afternoon when he told me he could get some. We snorkeled, rode the pedal boats, ate twice, napped, and chatted, but still no pot. Around seven I was getting irritated and every time I saw the guy, I kicked my chin up at him with the secret *What's up with what we talked about?* head jerk. He would say, "I get. I get. No worry."

I eventually gave up hope and settled into a cranky disappointment that my wife could not understand. I told her I was trying to get us all some pot and it didn't pan out. She was pissed that I hadn't told her earlier.

It was like one-thirty in the morning. It was our last night in the Middle East. I was lying outside on the ground, looking up at the stars of Egypt, festering about a pot deal that didn't go down, when I felt a tug on my arm. It was the little Arab guy. He said, "It is *time*."

I shook Kim, who had dozed off. I said, "Honey, it is *time*." Oriella was still awake, so she came with us. Jim was out cold. We followed the guy up a hill behind the hostel. On the top of the hill there were three women and four men sitting around a campfire talking and eating. They were passing around what looked like two hubcaps. One was filled with stew and the other with bread. The Arab guy told us it was chicken, and it had been cooking in the ground all day. We found an open place in the circle and sat beside the fire. The people greeted us in broken English. We were handed the hubcaps and we took some chicken with the bread and ate. It was delicious.

It became clear that no one could speak English, and I was getting antsy. Then one of the men took a bag of pot and a pouch of tobacco out of his pocket, dumped some of each into his hand, crumbled it, and rolled two large conical joints. The only other time I had seen joints that

looked like that was in the centerfold of *High Times* magazine when I was in high school. He lit one up and
started passing it around. The other he gave to our friend,
the little Arab guy, who then gave it to us. I lit it and took
a deep hit and passed to Kim. She took a hit. We got
really high.

Kim and Oriella tried to communicate with the others. One of the women knew Hebrew, so Oriella was able
to translate. It became a group effort to understand the
most mundane elements of life: Where are you from?
What's your name? What do you do? I sat and watched
the cinders crackle and float up lit into the pitch-black
sky and trail off as ashes. There was a timelessness to it.
The Middle East, Egypt, a campfire, Bedouins: It was
real Beat, primitive Beat, tribal. Whether there was a God
or not or which God it was if there was one didn't matter. There had always been people sitting around fires,
laughing and telling stories, intoxicated and alive, ex-
plaining who they were by making pictures with their
hands.

As dawn began to break we walked back down to the
hut. Oriella went to sleep. Kim sat down on the beach.
The sun was beginning to rise over Saudi Arabia. I took
off my Nikes and left them at the edge of the water and

walked out into the Red Sea. Everything about my life seemed so distant and unimportant, ridiculous. The sky was a pale purple, the mountains were humped shadows in the distance. I felt full, whole, beat. I looked down and saw my feet moving along the floor of the sea through the clear water.

14

IT'S been three years since I went to Israel. I no longer
have Jerusalem Syndrome. I found that the cure for it
was essentially living life. Nothing seems to have turned
out the way I thought it would.

Since the trip, I have separated from my wife. I have
given up smoking, drugs, and booze. I am no more Jewy
than I was before. I am painfully present most of the
time. Being on stage seems to be the only reprieve from
my insanity that I have left. I still believe there are no coincidences, but I no longer think I am the chosen one. I
think the path of my life has been to follow a trail of
crumbs being dropped unintentionally by a God eating a
piece of cake as he walks quickly away from a dinner I
wasn't invited to on his way to deal with the end of the
world.

I recently received a strange request. My mother's friend Rosalie called me. I have known her since I was a kid. "Marc, hi. It's Rosalie. How are you doing, sweetheart?"

"I'm fine. How are you?"

"Everything's great. I have a question for you. Would you be interested in coming to Albuquerque and performing a benefit for the synagogue?"

"I don't know. Why? What's going on?"

"Well," she said, "the temple isn't doing so well. The rabbi has Parkinson's, the cantor quit, membership is very low, and all the kids from your group are gone. Only the older people are left."

"Sounds sad," I said. "I don't know. It would be weird."

"Oh, come on, Marc. We thought it would be wonderful if you came out and did your routine," she said in that tone that made me realize I was being told that I *was* doing the show. "We could raise some money, give the congregation a little morale boost, and maybe some of your old friends would come out."

"I don't know. I need to check my schedule." I knew I had nothing on the books.

"We're also going to advertise in the paper so anyone can come," she said, still selling.

"Let me call you back." I wasn't sure if I wanted to do it.

"I need to know soon, honey," Rosalie said.

"Right, I'll call you back."

"Today, okay, sweetie?"

"Yes, yes, today. Bye."

I hadn't heard or even thought about Congregation B'nai Israel in at least fifteen years. I thought it over for a few minutes. It would be a free trip back to Albuquerque. It had been a long time since I had been back home. There was really no reason to go before, because my parents had split up and left there. I was excited. I would be able to see Gus and a few other people I had kept in touch with over the years. I could drive in the mountains. I called Rosalie back. "Yeah, I'll do it."

"Oh, great, everyone will be thrilled," she said, excited. She knew the deal was sealed before she even picked up the phone to call me the first time.

"Good," I said with some surrender in my voice.

"You just need to watch your language, and don't do anything raunchy. I know you can do that. For me, you'll do that."

I felt like I had just made a horrible but good decision. I really had no choice. It was the right thing to do.

When I flew to Albuquerque a few weeks later, I was

restless on the plane. I was overwhelmed with anxiety about performing at the synagogue. The picture that Rosalie had painted of the Jewish community I had grown up in was grim, and I began to think I couldn't pull it off. It all felt awkward and I wanted to go back to New York and forget about the whole thing.

When I arrived at the Albuquerque airport, I called Gus and asked him to meet me. I picked up my rental car and drove to the center of the universe, the Frontier Restaurant. I needed to ground myself. It had always worked in the past. It was an odd feeling to walk into a place that was so important to me at a time in my life that seemed so far behind me. The familiarity, the comfort—I walked around expecting to see someone I knew. Maybe I was expecting to see myself as I was in high school, sitting with my friends talking, smoking, and laughing. All of us full of the excited curiosity and bravado of acting jaded and being innocent. I did see some of the lunatics I knew as a kid still hanging around. That gave me hope.

Gus showed up and we caught up a bit. It was great to see him. We talked about movies, art, family, poetry, and what I had been doing. He said he was definitely coming to the show. That made me nervous. He had seen it advertised in the paper along with an article about me. It was the standard "hometown boy makes good, comes home to help" piece. I had a cheeseburger with green chilies on it and tried to relax. The interaction between us was different. It was the first time I really noticed that I wasn't some hyper, anxiety-ridden, insecure high school student looking for approval from someone I respected. I had changed. I was a hyper, anxiety-ridden, insecure adult looking for approval from someone I respected.

I left Gus and went to meet Rosalie at the synagogue. Driving around the streets of Albuquerque activated a grid of emotions in my heart and I moved through it. At every corner were ghosts of my experience, moments that had defined me. I could see the outside of Congregation B'nai Israel from a mile away because the roof of the sanctuary looked like the top of a large, opened, light brown umbrella. When I was growing up it was gray. Driving into the parking lot of the shul triggered all the memories of all the times I had arrived there as a kid for Hebrew school, for services, for my bar mitzvah. I walked in and was greeted by Rosalie. "Hi, sweetie. Everything okay?" She kissed me and smiled with her whole round face. Her hair was forever red. "You should look around. They renovated everything."

"Let's go over what's going to happen tomorrow night," I said, anxious.

We walked down the hallway to the social hall. Even
with the changes, everything seemed enough the same for
me to feel my childhood creeping out of every room of
the building. I walked by the classrooms where I threw
spitballs and wrote Hebrew on the blackboard. We
walked into the social hall where my friends and I would
do shots of Mogen David after services and smoke cigarettes with Herb out back. It was all fancy, with large tables and about two hundred place settings with flowers.
There was a podium set up and a screen.

"I can't do comedy at a podium. What's the screen
for?" I asked, panicking.

"Oh, didn't I tell you? We're having a fundraising dinner before the show for Marilyn Rienman in honor of her
service in the community. We thought you would emcee
it. You could pep it up. They're usually so boring. Did
you have Marilyn as a teacher?"

"Yeah, third grade, I think. She was one of the only
Hebrew school teachers I liked."

"See? This is going to be so wonderful," she said, sur-
veying the room. "Isn't it beautiful?"

"I wish you would have told me about the dinner. I
should prepare some stuff."

"You'll be fine," she said with mommy confidence.

"So, the show will be in here after the dinner?" I said, trying to figure out the logistics.

"No," she said frankly. "After dinner everyone will move up to the sanctuary for the comedy show."

"You want me to do comedy in the sanctuary?" I was freaking out a bit. "Is that okay? It seems like that would be wrong somehow. I'm not sure I'm comfortable with that."

"Look, you'll get comfortable. There are no other options. It'll have to be fine." She said this in that tone that suggested that there would be no other way to be other than fine.

"Do I have to wear a yarmulke?" I blurted.

"I don't know. I'll have to check with Mr. Ross."

"Mr. Ross is still here? Wow, yeah, you better check."

Mr. Ross was the brooding, bearded moral custodian of the synagogue. I'm not really sure what his job was, but he was always around when I was a kid. He acted as the bad cop to the rabbi's good cop. He was an authoritarian and a strict disciplinarian when it came to troublemakers, and the thought of him used to scare me.

"Marc, there are going to be two hundred people at the dinner and three hundred at the show. This is the biggest event of this kind we have ever had here. It's all because of *you*," Rosalie said, layering the guilt on top of the expectation beautifully; she was a real pro. "Just don't be filthy, sweetie," she said, and walked away to deal with the caterers.

I was momentarily terrified. I would be doing comedy on the same bema that I was bar mitzvahed on. I would do my jokes on the altar in front of the arc that contained the Torahs that I read from as a boy. It was too weird. It was almost as if I was getting a second chance to do it right. There was a moment when I thought I should actually read my haftorah. I had the same fear I had felt before my bar mitzvah, for roughly the same reasons.

I walked out of the social hall and up into the sanctuary alone. It wasn't much different than I remembered it. There was another panel of Yahrzeit plaques in the entrance, but aside from that it was pretty much the same. It was a large semicircular room with red carpet. About four hundred seats fanned out in sections around a semicircular bema that was elevated by two steps. There was a podium in the middle of the bema and a large arc behind the podium with chairs on each side. The roof was pitched, like the underside of a giant umbrella. In the center of the roof was a large circular skylight with a cylindrical lip cut at an angle that protruded into the room. It looked like the end of a giant organ pipe. A tube that light passed through. When I was a kid I thought that God listened through that hole.

I walked up the stairs and stood on the bema. The spiritual importance of the place had been hammered into my brain, so it felt holy. I vaguely remembered being up there and looking down at my Grandma Goldy smiling in the front row. My voice cracking through an over-studied adolescent rendition of the service. I stood alone in the quiet only a sanctuary can offer and I looked up, took a deep breath, and said, "God, I really need to get this out of the way. Forgive me." Then I yelled, "Fuck, shit, damn it, cock, pussy, motherfucker." I took another breath. "Look, I had to do that. I'm sorry. I don't want any of that coming out tomorrow night during the show. Save the old people some aggravation. You understand? That was between me and you, I, and thou, dig?" I felt relieved.

I walked out of the sanctuary and I was about to leave, but Rosalie stopped me. "The rabbi is in his office. He's been looking forward to seeing you," she said.

"Really? Right now?" I said. "I don't know. Is he alright?"

"He has his good days and his bad days. Today seems

to be a good day. He's on a new medicine that seems to work, but it makes his face somewhat expressionless." She walked me to the door of his office.

Rabbi Celnik was sitting at his desk, and when he saw me he stood up. I had forgotten he was like six foot five. He wasn't that old, maybe fifty-five. He had the same gray hair he always had, even when he was younger. He had a soft, friendly face and wore glasses. He walked over to me in the same peaceful, humble, warm lope I remembered as a kid when he walked up beside me as I prepared to read from the Torah. We shook hands.

"How are you?" he asked with no expression. "It's great to see you." I could see how he felt in his eyes. He was happy.

"Thanks. It's really great to see you too," I said. We sat down.

"Tell me what you've been up to," he said.

I had never really spoken to the rabbi as an adult before. I didn't know what to talk about, so I immediately started whining. I told him that my career wasn't working out the way I wanted it to. I told him about the end of my marriage. I told him about my family annoying me. I told him how it had been a rough year for me. I just blah-blah-blahed like a little baby. He listened and seemed to understand. I felt comforted by him even though I hadn't seen him in fifteen years.

I felt selfish, so I asked him how he was doing. He told me about his Parkinson's and how the new medicine he was on was helping. He told me about his new marriage. His first had ended after his wife had an affair with a member of the congregation. He told me that his new wife was ill with cancer but doing alright and that they had a beautiful new baby. He talked proudly about his older children from the first marriage. It was all very heartbreaking and bittersweet.

When I got up to leave he said, "What you do, Marc, provides a tremendous service to people. We are happy to have you here. You are performing a mitzvah by being here."

"Thanks. I'm glad I'm here," I said. "It's been really great talking to you." We shook hands.

"Before I leave," I said, "do you remember my haftorah?"

"Of course I do," he said. "It was Re'eh. It is a very beautiful one."

"Can you tell me what it's about, basically?"

"Basically," he said through the side of his mouth, "it's about having faith in the face of disappointment."

"How's your faith?" I said.

"Stronger than ever," he said, eyes smiling.

The night of the performance I was nervous. During the dinner I sat at a table with the rabbi and my old friends Dave and Steve, who had come to see me. I had known them since I was nine. We were all in Mrs. Reinman's class together. During the dinner Mr. Ross came up to me and whispered in my ear, "You will need to wear a kippa in the sanctuary."

I said, "Really?"

He shot me a look.

"Okay," I conceded, cowering.

When I stepped up to the podium I was overwhelmed by warmth. I felt love and loved. I looked out into the crowd and saw all the faces of the people that were grown-ups when I was a kid; they were all old. I felt as if I had been wandering for years and finally came home. Mrs. Reinman sat at the center table. Seeing her brought me back to a simpler time in my mind. A time when saying the Hebrew alphabet all the way through was a great accomplishment, and it was enough.

These people knew me when I was ten. I found that my feelings toward some of them were still the ones I felt at ten. There was Marilyn Bromberg, who was the president of the congregation when I was at my most mischievous. I spent a lot of time in her office being reprimanded. I saw her sitting in the crowd, a little older, but her power was intact. With her and Mr. Ross in the room I felt that I had better behave myself. The first thing I said at the dais was "It's been about fifteen years since I've been here and I still find Mr. Ross frightening." I got a huge laugh.

I introduced the rabbi, and he made his way to the podium. He wasn't moving as well as he had the day before. He was struggling a bit. He got up to the microphone and said, "It's amazing that Marc is doing the same thing he was doing here when he was a kid."

I interjected from the table, "Only now I won't be sent to Mrs. Bromberg's office."

Without missing a beat, the rabbi said, "Not yet." It brought the place down.

As I brought family members and friends up to pay tribute to Marilyn Reinman, I had a moment when I understood the power of the religious community. I imagined what it would feel like to try to obey the laws of God. To age, move through and share all the processes of life with a circle of people with common beliefs. To rally together and persevere in the face of adversity and evil. To help and hurt each other in the name of love. To be there for each other's successes, failures, joys, and tragedies, then to try to fill your heart with the good moments and elevate them to a true, deep feeling of worthiness as a human being. To know you've done the best you can in the eyes of your peers and in the eyes of God. Most important, to try to fight against that moment of horrible truth when you look around and realize how utterly unfair it all is, as the injustice of time and disease slowly levels everyone. That's where the idea of God really comes into play. It eases the move toward the ground. Believing in the grand plan can take the edge off if you let it, because it really doesn't end well for anyone. Acceptance.

After dinner, a parade of old Jews and a few younger ones moved toward the sanctuary, where there were already about a hundred people seated. They had purchased tickets for just the comedy show. Gus was there, as were many people I had known growing up. While everyone was getting settled in their seats I was in the lobby wrestling with the yarmulke no yarmulke dilemma. I understood it was a house of God and it was customary to wear a yarmulke, but I thought, *Why should I start following the rules now?* The only reason I was really concerned was out of respect for some of the older, more religious people and out of fear of Mr. Ross.

I decided against the yarmulke because I realized that even though they are my people, the ritual trappings of Judaism did not harness my idea of the Almighty. It was enough respect that I wouldn't be cussing. For one night God's house was my house, and I was going to work that house. I was there for a specific reason—to make people laugh—and I did. From the first joke through the last story I entertained the audience. I wasn't crass. I didn't cuss. I rode the edge just right, and I was true to myself. I thought, *That one was for my Grandma Goldy.*

After the show everyone was very excited. Gus was smiling when he walked up to me and said, "You were great." The evening had been a stellar success. Everyone had a good time and thirty thousand dollars was raised for the temple. I felt good about what I had done. Rosalie came up to me after the show beaming. "That was wonderful, sweetie. You were great. Everyone loved it."

"Great. Thanks. I think it went well," I said.

"Are you kidding? It was fabulous, and you know who loved it the most?" She was holding back the answer for a moment to let it build.

"Who?"

"The rabbi," she said, smiling. "Marc, no one has seen him laugh for two years, and he was hysterical."

That was all I needed to hear. Faith in the face of disappointment is only enhanced by laughter in the face of pain. That's my belief. That's my job. Whether it is a God-given talent or a reaction to something embedded in my heart I don't know, but it filled me with the heat of joy to hear that I made that connection, that I had that impact, that I provided that service, that I performed that mitzvah.

The last day I was home I took the rental car up old 14 behind the Sandia Mountains. As I drove north toward Santa Fe past Madrid I rolled the window down halfway and let the cold, brisk, February air come into the car. I smelled the piñon trees and the damp earth. The Gray came over me. My life flashed through my heart in one deep rush of feeling. When I made the turn around the mountain to the west, the mesas and valleys spread out before me under the orange and gold horizon. The sun hit me like a wave that flooded out the past and dissolved any idea of the future, and I felt okay and whole for about twenty minutes.

ACKNOWLEDGMENTS

THANK YOU, GERALD HOWARD, FOR GIVING me the opportunity to write this book and actually believing I could. Thank you, Kimberly Reiss, for being with me and loving me through most of the worst of it and some of the best of it. Thank you, Kirsten Ames, for codeveloping and directing the stage show that this book is based on and being with me through all that happened with that. Thank you, Sam Lipsyte, for being a true friend and guiding me through the process of writing like a writer writes. Thank you, Jack Boulware, for being the best running buddy I ever had. Thank you, Jim Loftus, for being Jim. Thank you, Craig Maron, for being my brother. Thank you, Devon Jackson, for being my oldest friend. Thank you, Mishna Wolff, for holding my hand when everything that I thought was true and real went away. Thank you, Jason Spiro, for the technical support that aided greatly in the creation of the stage show. Thank you, Roy Trejo, for illuminating me during the stage production of *Jerusalem Syndrome*. Thank you, Arnold Engelman, and the staff of the Westbeth Theatre Center for keeping me full of cigarettes, soda, and love. Thank you, Dave Becky and Michael O'Brien, for keeping the dream alive when I was a nightmare.